A History of
the Byfield Mine,
Combe Down

Richard T. A. Irving

A History of the Byfield Mine

First published in Great Britain 2005 by
The Combe Down Heritage Society
with assistance from Bath & North East
Somerset Council
Written by Richard T.A. Irving
Copyright © 2005 Richard T.A. Irving
Designed by Tiptoe Design
Printed by Emtone Print

ISBN 0-9550655-0-X

Contents

Tucked away in a quiet corner of my back garden there is a hole. It is an entrance - one of several around the village - to the Combe Down Stone Mines. Bats fly in and out of the hole, and occasionally we are asked to take part in a survey of their numbers by spreading a sheet to cover it. This encourages the bats to use another exit from the mine, where a research student sits quietly in the fading summer evening light to count them out, one by one.

A few years ago the hole was really a very small one. Anyone attempting to get in or out would have had to wriggle and squirm. I knew the hole must have been bigger in the past, and that over the years it had been filled with garden and other rubbish. Nevertheless the common assumption had been that the hole was too small to have allowed the extraction of large blocks of stone and that it must have been an entrance for the private use of the mine manager. I often wondered who this man might have been, but never really questioned why he should go to so much trouble to excavate a mere short-cut to his workplace. I naturally assumed that my house was, at some point in the past, the mine manager's house. The task I set myself at this time was, like that of so many other amateur historians, simply to discover the story of my house. Who built it, and who had lived in it over the years? Perhaps more unusually, I also wanted to know who had dug that hole in my garden.

One day a head popped out of the hole. It was Lynn Willies, consultant to the Stone Mines Project Team from Oxford Archaeology. I did not know it at the time but he is one of the foremost experts in the country on mine archaeology. I told him about the mine manager and his short-cut, joking that only a few weeks previously a staircase had been rediscovered leading underground from the King William IV pub. Now we knew where the real destination of the short-cut was! Lynn was not especially amused and gave me a look that suggested I really hadn't a clue what I was talking about. A few days later the layers of garden rubbish had been peeled away and Lynn was standing upright in the newly revealed arched entrance to the mine. It was indeed an inclined working entrance and, once upon a time, stone had been hauled out through this magnificent portal. In fact he considered it a highly significant feature of the Byfield complex, probably dating back to around 1800. It was clear I would have to re-think the history of the hole in my garden. This book is the product of those thoughts.

Lynn has since been more than willing to help me in my quest, and has read draft manuscripts at various stages, always offering prompt and invaluable commentary. My sincere thanks are due to him. Another constant source of help and guidance has been David Pollard, author of the first serious historical and archaeological assessment of the Combe Down stone mines in 1994. David has spent years researching the history of the quarries, both on the surface and underground. In many ways this book should really be his, since so much of it depends on the fruits of the time-consuming research he has done. David has been remarkably generous passing on to me the snippets of information he has gleaned from old newspapers and from places even deeper in the public archive. Just last week I received an e-mail from him telling me that he had come across an entry for Samuel and Ann Nowell in some obscure late 18th century marriage register. This book would simply not have been possible without David's constant and selfless help and encouragement.

In my own archival searches I, along with so many others before me, have been grateful for the ever-patient assistance of Colin Johnston and Lucy Powell at Bath City Archives. Likewise, my thanks to the staff at Somerset County Record Office in Taunton, and to Dr. Katherine Harris, Archivist to the Marquess of Bath at Longleat. Much new material has come to light in the deeds and documents belonging to local friends and neighbours. I am particularly grateful to Douglas and Nina Peters, Alan and Alison Garrett, Rosemary Simmons, and the late Lionel Simmons for letting me delve into their often musty, but always carefully preserved packages of parchment and papers. Special thanks are also due to Paul Deakin (FRPS) for his kind permission to reproduce photographs from his excellent collection of images of the underground workings.

My thanks are also due to Joy Nowell-Hill and to Patricia Griffin, both of whom provided information about their shared ancestor, Philip Nowell. There are many others who have assisted in a most valuable way by offering their advice or a recollection from the unwritten oral archive, or simply just an explanation of the workings of this - or that. Betty Lewis, Phil Bishop, David Morris, Margaret Todd, Malcolm Ayres, Jean Rendall, and the Barrow family - Dennis, Monica, Alan, and Susie, have all played a role in the writing of this book. So too have Lisa Pentreath, and my good friend Geoff Simmons - who lent me his camera and unfailing vocal support.

I am also extremely grateful to the Combe Down Heritage Society for their offer to publish this volume. During the time it has taken to research and write about the Byfield Mine local interest and support for heritage has grown to the extent that the Heritage Group, comprising a handful of members, has evolved into a fully fledged Society with membership in excess of a hundred. This is the first major publishing project to be supported by the Heritage Society and for that I am not just thankful but also greatly honoured.

My heartfelt thanks, and love, are due my family. All this work was done during the precious time I am at home with them. Their forbearance while I disappeared yet again down a dusty archive reflects the love and affection we share. Thank you Helen, Luke, John, and Eleanor.

I would dearly like to ascribe all possible instances of error, misrepresentation, and dissemination of false history to my erstwhile companions Lionel, Les, and Bob. Unfortunately I cannot. They have moved on and I must assume this responsibility alone. I do hope there are no mistakes, but I must stress the interpretations of sometimes ambiguous, sometimes incomplete data are entirely my fault. Instead, I dedicate this book to the memory of these dear friends, for they were with me all the time I thought about that hole in my garden.

Dick Irving,
Tor View,
March, 2005.

Foreword

It is a great privilege to be asked to write a foreword for the first book to be published by the Combe Down Heritage Society, particularly since the Combe Down mines have been one of the most important local issues during my time as an MP. Given the recent problems caused by the decaying infrastructure it would be easy to forget that stone quarried here has made an immeasurable contribution to the architectural splendour of the city, and to the heritage of the nation at large.

Dick Irving's book provides an important local perspective on the history of the mines. After all history is built on the experiences and testaments of ordinary people and Dick's book is all the more valuable for his personal and very literal connection to the mine. I hope the book is well received and that it contributes to the preservation of this most important chapter in Bath's history.

Don Foster MP
Liberal Democrat Shadow Secretary of State
for Culture, Media and Sport

Introduction

The 'mines' or 'underground stone quarries' at Combe Down are to be infilled in a project lasting many years and costing many millions of pounds. The purpose is to stabilise the undermined area to prevent subsidence and possible surface collapse. The safety and well-being of the people of Combe Down are of paramount concern, but a significant spin-off from the Stabilisation Project has been an increase in interest and awareness of the historical and cultural heritage associated with the mines. As far as most people are aware there are two mines in Combe Down - the Firs Mine and the Byfield Mine, although they are interconnected underground. At least, these are the names given by the Project team to the two sections of chambers, shafts and passageways which undermine an area of approximately 18 hectares of Combe Down village.

The Firs Mine is the larger of the two and, given its proximity to the centre of the village and Prior Park, is the one most often associated with Ralph Allen and the 'heyday' of stone quarrying in the 18th century. The Byfield Mine lies to the west of the village centre and so is rather removed from those features commonly linked with Ralph Allen; and it shares less of the limelight. In fact very little has been written about the Byfield Mine at all, compared with the volumes devoted to Ralph Allen's other enterprises (see Pollard, 1994, and Willies, 2002, for the most comprehensive summaries of the history of these Mines). In common with the Firs Mine, however, the recorded history of mining activities at Byfield in the post-Allen years appears vacuous, especially for the first half of the 19th century. After then modern company records and fragments of oral or other personal recollection shed some light on the decline and near demise of the stone industry in Combe Down (Beazer, 1981; Addison, 1998). The overall impression from this is that little in the way of innovation or involvement in major building projects occurred after the break-up of Ralph Allen's estate. This study attempts to correct this view, and argue that not only was the first half of the 19th century one of the most important and fascinating periods in the whole history of mining and quarrying in Combe Down, but that the Byfield Mine and adjacent area possibly led the way in providing Bath stone to a newly emerging national market. Ralph Allen may have provided the stone for the building of Bath, but it was the quarrymasters of Byfield who took the stone to so many country houses of the land, to the towering spires of Oxford, to the magnificent monuments of London, and to the palaces of the Kings and Queens of England.

The Byfield Mine

The names Firs Mine and Byfield Mine would almost certainly not have been familiar to Ralph Allen. Although an area known as 'the Firs', and quarries adjacent to it, are recorded from 1796 the name Byfield Mine was not coined until as late as the 1970s by Philip Wooster in an article entitled "The Stone Industry at Bath" (Wooster, 1978). He had noted that the stone mines at Combe Down, although interconnected, were formed in two distinct sections and that for the sake of convenience, if nothing else, it would be useful to name them as two distinct entities. He was also aware that throughout much of the history of stone quarrying in Combe Down there had been a myriad of masters, men, and miners whose names had been attached from time to time with various workings, both above and below ground. Addison (1998) has suggested identification for many of these (e.g. Street's quarry, Cox's Vertical Shaft Mine, Lankersheer's Quarry, not to mention Davidge's Bottom), together with other quarry and mine names associated with place (e.g. Greendown Quarries, Allotments Quarries, Lodge Style Quarries). Firs 'Quarry' (place) and Byfield Mine (name) are just two of a total of 41 areas of stone extraction recorded by Addison. Some of those on the list are distinctly separate entities, such as those at Odd Down and the ancient workings on Entry Hill, but many are part of or immediately adjacent to the Firs/Byfield complex and, indeed, a number of them are almost certainly double-counted. In other words, sometimes the same quarry goes under different names at different periods of time. Wooster's great contribution has been to simplify our reference of understanding of the undermined area.

The advantage of simplicity gained from the adoption of Wooster's nomenclature is necessarily offset by a loss of precision in our understanding of the evolution and development of the mines. The Firs Mine clearly takes its name from the plantations of Scotch Firs that Allen ordered to be planted on his estates around the time that the building of Prior Park was completed in the early 1740s. It is well known, however, that the mines and quarries had been operated from a much earlier period, and so originally they must have gone by some other name. In fact throughout the Allen years, and indeed for the rest of their operational lifetime, the quarries were generally referred to either as '*Mr. Allen's Free Stone Quarries*' (e.g. Thorpe, 1742) or, for example, '*the Stone Quarries*' or '*the Stone Quarrys on Comb Down*', or the '*Combe Down Quarry*' (e.g. Somerset CRO DD/X/LA 12, and Somerset CRO D/T/ba 36). After the eventual break-up of the estate in 1803, following the death of Lord Hawarden (formerly known as Earl de Montalt), surviving individual quarries tended to be known by the name of the local quarrymaster. Davidge's Bottom is so named, though it was actually one of the original quarries on the Down operated by Ralph Allen. Even throughout the whole of the 19th century there seems to be no specific reference to the Firs Quarry, or Mine, described by both Wooster and Addison, although the 1851 Tithe Apportionment for Monkton Combe does describe the occasional '*quarry and plantation*'. The area known today as Firs Field was called '*The Park*' in 1851, and even when this was sold as part of the Hadley Estate in 1901 it was described simply as '*Pasture land*'. The firs had long since been cut down!

The Byfield Mine takes its name from the fact that one of the three entrances to the former underground workings at this site is situated adjacent to Byfield Place and Byfield Buildings, near the junction of Combe Road and Summer Lane. These places are named after a certain James Byfield who, in a deed of 1825, is described as a '*haullier*' of Bath. The 1841 Census records his wife (widow), Mariah, aged 55, living at 6 Byfield Place. For a while James Byfield did indeed become quarrymaster, but he was hugely unsuccessful and accumulated massive debt. Clearly his 'Allenesque' attempt to achieve full vertical integration of the stone business did not work, and he died, presumably, a broken man. More of James Byfield later in this story. Meanwhile, the mine which bears his name can claim a more distinguished history. Archaeological evidence confirms that its origins date back at least as far as the quarrying activities of Ralph Allen (Willies, 2002), and historical documentation suggests association with other well known quarrymasters such as the Lankesheers, William Hulonce (senior and junior), Henry Street (also senior and junior), at least one of the Sumsions, and the enormously successful Nowell family.

The relative paucity of historical documentation for the post-Allen years is often cited as the main reason why so little is known about the evolution of the industry in the late 18th and early 19th centuries. One problem, possibly, is that too much attention has been focused on the underground workings compared to the extensive surrounding areas of surface quarry. It seems likely that at least some quarrymasters were able, with equal confidence, to work above as well as below ground. The extent of the old underground workings can be determined today by simply tracing the voids left under the surface (though extensive backfilling renders this task more difficult in some places). Tracing the area of old surface quarry workings is not always so easy, however, especially in areas where quarries have been filled back up to the original surface level, and subsequently built upon. From the information that can be gleaned, especially now that this has been augmented by the results of bore-hole surveys for the Stabilization Project, it seems that the area of surface quarrying in Combe Down was actually more extensive than the 'mined' area (Oxford Archaeology, 2004). In other words, in order to supplement our knowledge of the post-Allen quarrymasters we need perhaps to cast the net over a wider area than has been studied until now.

The second reason for the apparent paucity of information is that, quite simply, researchers have not been looking in all the right places. An oft neglected fact is that the morphological entity we recognise today as Combe Down Village spans an area that originally comprised parts of two parishes. When, in Ralph Allen's day, the seeds of the village first took root the first houses (de Montalt Place) were built adjacent to the quarries in the north-west corner of Monkton Combe parish. When quarrying activity expanded - following the line of natural rock outcrops - the trail led quarry workers and their families across the parish boundary to settle in a remote corner of the equally ancient Lyncombe and Widcombe Parish. Baptismal records for those families who had settled on the other side of the parish line in the early 19th century are very clear in describing residence as being, for example, in the Widcombe part of Combe Down.

In terms of the modern landscape the parish boundary followed the line of Combe Road south to Rock Hall Lane. Here, at Ralph Allen's Yard (formerly Gammon's Yard), the boundary veers east, behind Rock Hall Cottages, and heads down the slope into Horsecombe Vale. Adjacent to the boundary at this point is Byfield Place and one of the entrances to the Byfield Mine. Overlaying the line of the parish boundary on a map of the mines shows clearly that Firs Mine is associated with Monkton Combe Parish whereas the Byfield Mine straddles the boundary with Lyncombe and Widcombe Parish (fig.1). In the 1980s, when the first attempts were made to make an accurate survey of all the underground workings associated with Combe Down, the caverns were grouped into 'sectors' for convenience of recording and reference. The sectors do not necessarily bear any relation to the different individuals who might have opened up and worked the underground quarries. As far as Byfield is concerned, the larger part of the mined area, incorporating Sectors P, Q, R, T, and X, is on the

Monkton Combe side of the parish boundary (Pollard, 1994). Sector S is on the Lyncombe and Widcombe side, and recent bore-hole survey work has confirmed the existence of extensive areas of former open quarry which almost completely surround the undermined area on this side of the boundary. Documentary research confirms that these quarries were an integral part of the Byfield complex, and that stone extraction continued well into the 19th century. Fortunately this apparently forgotten corner of Combe Down is well documented, since Lyncombe and Widcombe Parish records have survived generally intact compared to the rather fragmentary information available for the Monkton Combe side of Combe Down. Thus the history of the Byfield Mine is indeed open to scrutiny within the public archive, with reference to the post-Allen quarrymasters in particular.

If the associated former surface quarry workings are taken together with the underground sections of quarry it is clear that most of the Byfield 'Mine' lies within an area which was formerly part of Lyncombe and Widcombe parish. The oldest of the former entrances to the mined area, dating back to the time of Ralph Allen, is located near Byfield Place (Willies, 2002). In fact this site (now known, and hereafter referred to as Ralph Allen's Yard) has a small cluster of entrances, although the precise arrangement of them is difficult to know since they have long since been blocked up. These entrances lie close to the old parish line (a parish boundary marker can still be seen in the wall of the yard buildings), but are all actually on the Monkton Combe side. Although an underground 'wall' (an unquarried section of stone) divides the underground sectors for much of the length of the parish boundary at least one of these entrances gave direct access to both sides (i.e. to Sectors S and T). For the sake of clarity in this study it is useful to add prefixes to the name 'Byfield Mine' whenever it is necessary to distinguish the area of quarry workings under discussion. Adoption of 'LW Byfield' and 'MC Byfield' should be self evident. Since much of the documentary record is from Lyncombe and Widcombe Parish archives much of the attention in this study will inevitably focus on LW Byfield.

The Byfield Quarrymasters I

Among the records for which the Lyncombe and Widcombe archives are particularly rich are sets of deeds, maps, and other documents related to the land acquisitions of Magdalene Hospital and Bruton Hospital since their respective foundations many centuries ago. Magdalene Hospital deeds are for the greater part found in the St Johns Hospital Archive, managed by and accessible through Bath City Archives. Of special importance in this collection are documents relating to Rock Hall - the house built by Philip Nowell, for his retirement, on land formerly quarried by his family. Bruton Hospital records are maintained at Somerset County Record Office (Somerset CRO) and include a map showing the estates of all land holders in Lyncombe and Widcombe in the crucial year of 1799.

Another very important set of documents is the Parish Rate Books for Lyncombe and Widcombe which exist in a continuous series from the year 1796, and which are also held in Bath City Archives. In the years following Lord Hawarden's death in 1803 the Rate Books suggest that the land now associated with the LW Byfield Mine had been bought by Harry Salmon and divided into six lots for resale to men who could exploit the land for its valuable stone. Salmon even laid out plans for new roads to serve the quarrying activities, though only a short stretch of road was ever built. (The Allen Estate Map – see below – suggests these 'intended' roads were pre-existing rights of way. Presumably Salmon's intention was merely to widen them – to make them fit for the transport of stone.) By 1804 the six successful lessees/purchasers are named, and the rates charged for their quarrying activities are ascribed. The six are: Henry Street (Snr); John Scrace; Abraham Sumsion; William Hulonce (Snr); Jonathan Rudman; and Samuel Nowell. These men, together with the Lankesheers (James and Richard) of MC Byfield are the known quarrymasters of the Byfield Mine at this time.

It is odd that not one of these names today strikes a familiar chord – at least, not in the way that the name of Ralph Allen is so easily recalled through his various legacies. Did these men lack the verve and foresight of Allen, to buy up the whole Combe Down quarry operation and so corner the market for Bath stone? Could they not at least band together to construct a simple railway, as Allen had done, to transport the stone cheaply and efficiently to the market site? Did they strive for efficiency through competition with one another? Were they simple miners/quarrymen, perhaps survivors from Allen's time (he died in 1764), who merely lacked the capital or entrepreneurial insight to succeed? Indeed, who exactly were these quarrymasters of the early 19th century?

The answer is that these were men of a new age, who approached stone quarrying in a totally different manner to Ralph Allen. He, together with architect friends, had dreamed up ideas for a new urban form. Their dreams began with the creation of a new Bath town, the richness of form and substance overflowing, via new inland waterway navigation systems, to Bristol, London, and beyond. Ralph Allen was to be the provider of substance – the stone – Bath stone – at a price and a quality that had never before been bettered. He would quarry the stone and work it into rough blocks at Combe Down. He would then transport the blocks along a specially designed railway to Dolemeads (in modern Widcombe village), beside the river near the centre of Bath, where masons would work the stone to architects/builders specifications. Builders (masons) then made arrangements for the collection or delivery of the stone, and carried on the process of urban renewal from that point.

Forty years after Allen's death the new quarrymasters of Combe Down were the builders themselves (and, it must be said, Ralph Allen was an entrepreneur who only rarely, if ever, dirtied his hands cutting and sawing, let alone transporting blocks of stone), and it is they who developed the means to complete the process of vertical integration merely envisaged by Allen. True, most of these quarrymasters seemed to concentrate on the building project in hand and perhaps lacked the wider dreams and visions of Ralph Allen in terms of constructing a new urban landscape in metropolitan England. Yet, from the ranks of this small group of *builders* came a man who not only appears to have quarried on a scale matching Ralph Allen, but constructed buildings which, in total, have enhanced the architectural legacy of England to a much greater degree than Allen's relatively modest achievements. This man was Philip Nowell, son of the aforementioned Samuel Nowell, and son-in-law to Henry Street (Jnr). At the time of his death in 1853 this self-confessed '*former tradesman*' owned all surviving fragments of the LW Byfield Mine.

Green Down, Late Collibees Down, or Quarr Down?

Deeds and other legal documents referring to the sites covered by the LW Byfield Mine refer to the original name as, typically, "... *a certain piece or inclosure of ground formerly called Collibees Green Down or Quarr Down situate in the parish of Lyncombe and Widcomb ...*". Green Down was clearly the ancient name by which this particular stretch of ridge top was known. Further west, Green Down became Odwood Down – modern day Odd Down. To the east, in Monkton Combe Parish, the name was '*Sleights Hills and Mountains*' - a name suggesting that sheep grazing was the predominant activity (Somerset CRO DD/X/LA 12, and also Willies, 2002). In fact, according to OED, 'sheep sleights' is a local dialect term implying the *right* of sheep-herders to graze their flocks on common pasture. Indeed, the very simplicity of these names, all in general use in the early 1700s locally, suggests that most of the Down was common land, for the use of all local people, irrespective of profession or status. Commons enclosure by a series of Private Acts of Parliament in the 18th century allowed local landowners to 'steal the common off the goose' - as contemporary rhymers phrased it – and so enlarge their holdings at the expense of the 'commoner'. Although further research on this intriguing topic is required for the Combe Down area, it is entirely reasonable to speculate that Edward Collibee was one such petitioner for a 'Private Act'. The fact that Collibees Green Down, an area of 58 acres, is described as an 'inclosure of ground' adds credence to this view. To carry speculation a little further, it is entirely plausible that Ralph Allen's somewhat secretive acquisition of 'Sleights Hills' in the 1720s was carried out in collusion with other landowners, such as Collibee, in order to transform the land from traditional pasturage to industrial quarrying.

According to Addison, Collibees Green Down was subsequently sold to the Duke of Kingston and later to Ralph Allen and the Prior Park Estate (Addison, 1998; 43-44), and so the enclosure was usually referred to as 'late Collibees' in the sense that the land had formerly belonged to Collibee. This extensive tract extended both sides of the Bradford Road, but the section relevant to the Byfield Mine was the nineteen or so acres south of the road. This was the site, bounded at its northern end by modern Greendown Place, Bradford Road, and Combe Road, that later acquired the alternative name of Quarr(y) Down. Crucial to any understanding of the history of the Byfield Mine is to discover when this renaming occurred.

The earliest extant documentary records of quarries in Lyncombe and Widcombe go back to the 16th century. Particularly intriguing is a manuscript reference dated 1580 in the Bruton Hospital archive to the lease of a stone quarry in Lyncombe and Widcombe parish called *'le olde quarre'* (Somerset CRO DD/SE 28). This, however, almost certainly refers to the ancient workings on Entry Hill and, although close to other Collibee properties in the late 18th century, has no relation to the Byfield Mine. An early reference to Quarry Down is found within a summary of rentals of farms and lands of Lord Viscount Hawarden in 1795, a few years after he had inherited the Prior Park Estate. The record describes Mr. Edward Willis as tenant of *'One other Close residue of Collibees late Green Down* [sic] *now called Quarry Down and is South of the Turnpike Road'*. The area of this property is given as 18 acres, 3 roods, and 39 perches (Somerset CRO DD/X/LA 12). The tone suggests the change of name had been fairly recent, but in the absence of earlier dateable manuscripts it is hard to clarify exactly when this happened. Evidence gleaned from contemporary maps may prove useful, however.

Thomas Thorpe's survey of 1742 is often cited for the useful information it provides on the extent and scale of *'Mr Allens Free Stone Quarry'* (fig. 2). Of particular interest here is the line of the road leading to Combe (i.e. Monkton Combe). A completely different course is followed at the northern end to that of modern day Combe Road. Instead, Thorpe's route coincides more or less with the old 'drungway' leading from North Road to Davidges Bottom, passing the site of the first of Allen's three quarries. It then skirts around to the second quarry, descending through the outcrop to pass by the foot of the workings. Facility for the drying and storage of cut stone appear to have been available here in a large 'yard'. This gives the appearance that this quarry was, at the time of Thorpe's survey, the most important of Allen's workings. It is somewhat ironic to note, therefore, that this is the site of the entrance to the Byfield Mine, as it is known today, and that the yard in question is in the area of Byfield Place and the appropriately renamed 'Ralph Allen's Yard' (Wooster, 1978; 8). In fact, archaeological evidence now confirms that Allen's underground workings were probably more extensive here than any other site on the Down at this time (Oxford Archaeology, 2004).

Thorpe's survey does not show the parish boundary, and the field boundary pattern seems to approximate only very roughly with the line which later delineates Quarry Down. Forty five years later, in 1787, a survey of Bath's Turnpike Roads highlights the remarkable extent to which the landscape in this area had changed after the time of Thorpe's map (Somerset CRO D/T/Ba 24). It is a beautifully crafted, hand painted series of maps surveyed by Charles Masters, but all the maps are in strip-form designed to show the state of the turnpikes and ownership of the fields immediately adjacent. Not all Combe Down is shown, therefore. Most importantly, it shows that the road 'To Combe' had been moved to the modern day (Combe Road) location, where the parish boundary is also clearly marked (fig. 3). This realignment (by no means a minor project) seems to have been carried out under the instructions of Ralph Allen to facilitate enlargement of his fir plantations. The nascent forest evident in Thorpe's map is now seen to be a mature plantation extending all the way from The Avenue to Combe Road, implying that most planting took place in the mid to late 1740s, and that modern Combe Road was laid out at the same time. Also of interest are two open quarries shown just to the east of the Firs plantation, and a small quarry on the north side of the Turnpike at Crossway Place. Nearby, at the top of Entry Hill a separate sheet shows two more quarries, also opened up since Thorpe's map of 1742. Boundaries corresponding to 'Quarr Down' are shown clearly on Masters' survey, but no indication is given of any stone quarrying there.

The delineation of 'Quarr Down' is most clearly shown on a map dated 1799, commissioned by the Trustees of Bruton Hospital to show the extent of their land holdings in Lyncombe and Widcombe parish as well as the holdings of all other land owners in the parish (Somerset CRO LW map, 1799). The surveyor was J. Charlton (Chapman, Hawkes and Holland, 1998). Field and property boundaries are marked with great precision, individual houses are shown, and the acreages of all enclosures are clearly labeled. So too are the names of the owners of all the plots, as well as the names of the larger fields. There are even indications of the land use of a number of sites including, for example, 'Poorhouse' and 'Workhouse Garden' and, significantly, a number of 'quarries' are labelled. A very small quarry is indicated along the southern edge of the present area of interest, but this is far down the slopes of Horsecombe Vale and seems most unlikely to have given rise to the name 'Quarr Down' - although it may help throw light on earlier quarrying activity in this area (see Pollard, 1994). Indeed Quarr Down is merely referred to by its former names: 'Green Down – Late Collibees'. The owner is given as Lord Hawarden and the acreage as 17 acres,

2 roods for the greater part of the enclosure, with a smaller fenced section surrounding a further 2 acres, 2 roods, and 20 perches (fig. 4). Unfortunately, the Apportionments Schedule, which should give indication of the actual occupiers of the land, is missing. On the positive side, however, there are features shown on the map which are highly suggestive of an unfolding development – of quarrying activity which is just in the process of becoming a major feature of the local landscape.

The shape and position of the smaller enclosure is particularly intriguing. It resembles a bite-shaped 'chunk' in the area where Rock Hall Lane now exists. The fence which surrounds the enclosure continues across the parish boundary into Monkton Combe – a transgression not repeated anywhere else on the map. The shape suggests quarrying may be going on and the adjacent 'Byfield Mine', at Ralph Allen's Yard, would seem to be the likely source of this activity. Strangely, the parish boundary here, and here alone, is represented by a hatched line. Such lines are employed elsewhere on the map, and seem to represent the transient visible boundaries of quarries, the Entry Hill complex being a particularly good example. The suggestion is that, by 1799, quarrymen from the MC Byfield Mine had marked out the extent of their interest in the downland on the far side of the parish boundary by building a stone fence. Perhaps the fence served as a marker of the intended extent of the quarry, or perhaps it marked the *de facto* quarry edge.

There is another map which should, in theory, help clarify our understanding of the process of transition from the 1742 landscape to those of 1787 and 1799. In fact, in theory, it should be our primary source of reference for this period. It is the *"Survey of the Manours of Hampton, Claverton with Widcombe belonging to Ralph Allen Esqr."* held in Bath City Archives. This substantial, but highly enigmatic map has been described in some detail by Mike Chapman (1996). To paraphrase Chapman's observations: this large, undated map, drawn at a scale sufficient to show small details such as field-gates, was drawn principally for display (i.e. to show-off); the original surveyor was Thomas Thorpe, but the only existing version is probably a composite of several maps drawn between the 1740s and the 1760s; the map, though now conserved, is in a battered (somewhat incomplete) state, but is accompanied by a series of schedules providing details of land-use and occupancy.

The main difficulties regarding interpretation of Allen's Estate Map lie with establishing the date of survey and the intended purpose of the final drawing, particularly with regard to Allen's estates on the 'Down'. A number of features highlighted on Thorpe's 1742 survey are apparent, including the quarrymen's cottages (de Montalt Place) built in 1729, and the sites of two of the original three horse-crane housings (fig. 5). The modern line of Combe Road is shown, however, and the patently obvious fir plantation is well established, so this section of the map must post-date the mid-1740s at the earliest. Most surprisingly, the quarries and stone mines are barely shown at all – with the exception of the crane sites. The notion that this is because stone extraction was essentially an underground activity is barely sustainable, particularly if the scene facing de Montalt cottages is compared to that sketched by Thomas Robins in 1759. Robin's drawing, now in the collections of the Victoria Art Gallery in Bath, shows a crane house atop a sharp quarry edge, with clear ground behind it as far as the row of cottages. The Estate Map indicates that about half of this open ground has been forested, and that no obvious trace remains of the quarry. If both views are accurate (and if the Robins sketch is accurately dated) the only conclusion can be that this section of the Estate Map was completed (amended) near the time of Allen's death in 1764.

Other evidence exists to fuel this mystery. First, following Allen's death all equipment relating to stone extraction was sold off quickly. The beneficiaries of the Estate apparently had no interest in maintaining an active role in quarrying and sold off related assets to cover debts they faced regarding other aspects of Allen's beneficence (Boyce, 1967). This may have been a response to national economic recession at the time, when the King's army and naval forces were becoming increasingly stretched in conflicts around the World; whatever, the Estate Map suggests assets were already being stripped and that the mines faced possible closure. Chapman notes, in fact, that a surveying bill was paid to Capability Brown after Allen's death, possibly to pay for revisions to the Map (Chapman, 1996; 2). Such revisions could, conceivably, have included the addition of more fir trees than actually existed at the time to suggest plans for a change in land-use – a change that would presumably add to the value of the estate. Later, Earl de Montalt did indeed alter the character of Combe Down by promoting its remodeled attractions to the genteel classes who might seek the fresh air and fine south facing aspect of the Down after partaking of the spa waters in Bath for health reasons. The Estate Map seems much more in keeping with Mr. Rack's observations of 1780 than with images of rural industry conjured from Allen's day:

The beautiful and extensive prospect, the wild but pleasing irregularities of the scenery, the extensive plantations of fir, which throw a solemn gloominess of shade, impervious to the sun and the winds, over a fine, soft turf, free from underwood - all serve to render it a delightful summer retreat.

(quoted in Rambles About Bath and its Neighbourhood, 1889).

It is not actually certain that stone quarrying did continue uninterrupted on the Down after Allen's death, though any cessation must have been only temporary. The respective locations of de Montalt Cottages, built at the beginning of Allen's quarrying activity in 1729, and of the three crane sites shown on the 1742 map by Thorpe would seem to suggest the following historical sequence of stone extraction, which initially focused on an open quarry site just south of the cottages. The final line of this quarry face still can be seen behind Quarryvale Cottages, although the area of stone extracted would have extended at least as far as present day Summer Lane. This is the quarry illustrated in Robin's sketch of 1759. Quarrying soon extended westwards along the outcrop, creating a sizeable indentation in the area later known as Davidge's Bottom – though it is possible this was a quarry predating Allen. This was the second site for a horse-crane on Thorpe's map, and became a major access point to the underground quarries later known as Firs Mine. Small exploratory workings were probably dug along the whole face of the outcrop until another deep access point to underground workings was excavated near Byfield Place, into the so-called Byfield Mine. This was the site of the third crane, and also of what appears to be a large stone drying and cutting yard, according to the 1742 map. The location of this last entrance is of great interest because it is immediately adjacent to the parish boundary. This was the apparent limit of Allen's lands, and of the earliest phase of his stone quarrying activity.

The owner of the Widcombe land, on the other side of the parish boundary, was the Duke of Kingston. According to Addison he had purchased it from Collibee in the 1720s (- was this possibly part of a deal where the sale was offered in return for the Duke's support in Parliament for a private Act of Enclosure?). The land, known as 'late Collibees' or 'Green Down' was sold to Allen in 1744, at a time, presumably, when Allen's exploratory quarrying suggested the time was right to continue westward expansion along the outcrop into Widcombe parish. The purchase also must have facilitated Allen's plan to move Combe Road to the line of the parish boundary and so consolidate his fir plantations. Once the land was acquired quarrying could be extended across the boundary, both above and below ground. Indeed, this situation is reflected in the Allen Estate Map which shows a crescent shaped clearing in the plantations in the area of Ralph Allen's Yard. The clearing is bisected by the parish boundary, with the western half located in Widcombe parish. This pattern is reflected precisely in the 1799 Bruton Map, where the Widcombe section of quarry equates with the 'bite-shaped chunk' of land in *Green Down – late Collibees*. The schedule attached to the Allen Estate Map confirms this is *'quarry ground'*; in fact this reference is one of the few firm indications provided in these sources that quarrying ever took place on Allen's estates! Whether or not quarrying was still going on at the time the schedule was written is a moot point, since the date (1741) on one copy of the schedule is open to question and another copy, just like the map itself, is undated. Nevertheless, it now seems safe to conclude that the name 'Quarr Down' was acquired some time shortly after Allen's purchase of this land in 1744.

It is useful at this point to summarize the information that can be gleaned from these various sources. During the 1720s and 1730s Allen established, then expanded his quarrying activity – moving the main workings both westward and underground. The Byfield Mine (i.e. MC Byfield) was established towards the end of this period, and by 1742 had become the main site of operation. Exploited as an underground quarry, the workings extended along 'roadways' driven in a northerly and a north-easterly direction from two adjacent entrances in Ralph Allen's Yard. Underground penetration extended further than at any other of Allen's quarry sites, and so shafts were later excavated above the face workings to facilitate extraction of the stone blocks as well as provide ventilation. This technique was also evident later in the Firs Mine. Expansion westward was continued when, in 1744, Allen purchased all or part of 'late Collibees Green Down'. Combe Road was constructed, possibly to facilitate the movement of stone from these expanded workings, although the actual extent of these workings seems to have covered no more than two acres of Widcombe Parish. At the time of Allen's death in 1764 the market for stone was in decline and Allen's successor to his estates – Earl de Montalt (later Lord Hawarden) – sought alternative land-uses. The Estate Map was revised to reflect the diminished importance of quarrying. The revision perhaps also reflects de Montalt's real motives: to consolidate, if not expand the area of his Estate.

The Widcombe Field Quarry

In 1796 a *'measurement'* and valuation of quarries was made by Charles Masters for the Trustees of the Bath Turnpike Roads (Somerset CRO D/T/ba 36). Even if quarrying had gone through difficult times following the death of Ralph Allen, possibly ceasing temporarily at some sites, it is clear that by the time of Masters' survey stone was once again ringing to the sound of the jadding pick. Lord Hawarden's (i.e. de Montalt's) lands are shown to have included at least two quarries: *'Coomb Down Quarry'*, valued at one pound sterling per acre; and *'Widcombe Field Quarry'*, valued at just ten shillings. Other quarries, belonging to other owners, are highlighted, including *'Entry Hill Quarry'* (owned by Bennett Esq. and valued at one pound five shillings), and land quarried on the *'west side'* of the Rev'd. Smith's estate *'near the Firs'*, valued at ten shillings per acre. It has already been established that Lord Hawarden owned quarries on both sides of the parish boundary, in Monkton Combe and in Lyncombe and Widcombe, but where exactly was the 'Widcombe Field Quarry'? Was it the same place as Quarr Down?

The 1799 Bruton map contends that Widcombe Field was 56 acres of un-owned land, implying that it was still 'common' in the last years of the 18th century. This area covers, more or less, the site of the modern Foxhill Estate. The map acknowledges, on the other hand, that Lord Hawarden owned 14 acres of land just to the west of Foxhill Lane which, delineated by a solid line, was called *'Part of Widcombe Field'*. The Allen Estate Map suggests that almost all the land between Combe Down and Odd Down (including Widcombe Field) had been the property of, or had been leased to Ralph Allen, and so would now be in the possession of Lord Hawarden. The extension of the fir plantations along the sides of the Turnpike (Bradford Road), shown in both the Estate Map and the 1787 Turnpike Map, would seem to substantiate this claim, though it is of course possible these trees were planted after Allen's death, perhaps by Capability Brown, in an attempt to pre-empt any claim by others. What seems apparent is that a dispute did exist concerning the ownership of parts of the (former) common, a dispute which presumably focused on the various acquisitions Allen made between 1724 and 1744 and the actual extent of the original Parliamentary Enclosure(s). These purchases could have involved 'late Collibees' land, or perhaps the earlier acquisition of Dr Ponters Estate which, according to Richard Jones (Allen's Clerk of Works), reached almost to Odd Down (Wooster, 1978; 8). The trustees of Bruton Hospital certainly did not recognize the claim of Lord Hawarden; indeed, the 1799 map may well have been commissioned as part of their response to this dispute. The fascinating notion that the Allen estates were acquired by a combination of somewhat dubious and downright illegal acquisitions is one that demands further research. For the moment, however, this narrative must return to the question of the Widcombe Field Quarry, and the evidence offered in the 1799 Bruton map.

Although the Bruton map indicates a number of quarries, none are shown in the areas named 'Widcombe Field' (un-owned) and 'Part of Widcombe Field' (Lord Hawarden). Where quarrying is shown clearly to exist, such as at the top of Entry Hill and at Crossway Place, the land belongs to people other than Lord Hawarden and this fact appears not to be disputed in the Allen Estate Map. On the south side of the Bradford Road an extension of the former Green Down is called, simply, '*Down Field*' - an area of just over 12 acres. At the east end of Down Field a hatched line marks a new, possibly temporary boundary of land which adjoins 'Late Collibees' (i.e. 'Quarr Down') and which *is* shown to be under the ownership of Lord Hawarden (fig. 4). The fact that Hawarden's name is associated with these two acres of land, but is not so clearly associated with the remainder of Down Field suggests dispute also existed concerning this part of the common too. A deed of 1805 identifies this two acre strip as '*Great Barn Ground*' (Bath City Archives MH/7/14) which means it was almost certainly part of a wider area of land also occupied by Willis in 1795. (Willis appears to have been Hawarden's chief tenant on the Down; his tenancy included Quarr Down as well as 82 acres in Monkton Combe – including the former 'Sleights Hills' and the quarries there). A description of the 'Green Down' part of Willis' tenancy is contained in the 1795 rental book of Hawarden's farms and lands: '*Two Closes of Green Down formerly one Inclosure and anciently parcel of Green Down on Comb Down with a barn on some part thereof late Smiths*' (Somerset CRO DD/X/LA 12). The combined area of these 'Two Closes' is given as just over 31 acres; an area substantially larger than Down Field by itself. A number of adjoining fields or 'closes' (i.e. enclosures) could be added in order to tally the figures, including '*Wall Tyning*' to the west, or possibly '*Part of Widcombe Field*' to the north, on the other side of the Bradford Road, but we do not know yet for certain the precise extent of the Willis tenancy.

None of this evidence is conclusive, but the fact that 'Widcombe Field' appears to have been common suggests the name may have been interchangeable with 'Green Down' in some cases. The 1795 rental book demonstrates that 'Green Down' was interchangeable with 'Comb Down' when applied to Monkton Combe parish, so it may be that 'Widcombe Field' was used by some to refer to land on the Lyncombe and Widcombe side of 'Green Down'. Although this argument remains tenuous it does at least suggest a connection between the names Quarry Down and Widcombe Field Quarry, implying that they could indeed be the same place. It seems more likely, however, that they were separate entities. Quarr Down, even though it was just inside Lyncombe and Widcombe, was associated with the former Ralph Allen quarries in Combe Down. In any case, great care is always taken to refer to this plot also as 'late Collibees'. Furthermore, there is additional evidence to suggest that Widcombe Field Quarry may have been located in that two acre plot ('Great Barn Ground'), agreed by all to belong to Lord Hawarden, immediately adjacent to Quarr Down. If this is so, the quarry forms an important and integral part in the story of the development of the Byfield Mine.

The rental books for the Hawarden estates between 1795 and 1798 also contain a list of rentals for 14 Stone Quarries on 'Comb Down' (Pollard, 1994; 10-11). In effect, this means that at least fourteen individuals had secured the right to extract stone from designated sections of existing surface or underground quarry faces. The names of the tenants appear to be arranged in random order, although it is reasonable to assume that they could be listed in the sequence of the locations each one worked. If that is the case, on the basis of known associations of five of the quarrymasters (Singers, Lankesheer, Noel, Hulance, and Rudman) with the Byfield Mine after 1804, it may be reasonable to conclude that the first 8 of the 14 listed quarries were worked from the area around Ralph Allen's Yard. Of the remainder, some must have quarried at Davidges Bottom since this area was known to have been in operation until at least 1841. Could just a few of the remaining tenant quarrymasters on this list have worked the Widcombe Field Quarry?

This assertion can be checked by referring to entries in the Lyncombe and Widcombe Parish Rate Books after 1796. Unfortunately, no match with any of the quarrymasters listed in the Hawarden accounts is revealed – except Samuel Noel (Nowell), who is shown to be erstwhile owner of a property in the newly erected Devonshire Buildings on Wellsway (indicating that he was very likely the builder of this significant suburban development). In fact only one quarrymaster is listed as paying rates for his quarrying activity, and he is not included in the Hawarden rent accounts. His name is Henry Street, who, according to later, more detailed entries in the Rate Books, lived at Crossway Place (on the north side of Bradford

Road, just east of the junction with Entry Hill). It would seem, on the face of this evidence, that the quarryman at the top of Entry Hill, on lands not owned by Hawarden, can be identified, but that we are no closer to knowing the quarrymen of 'Widcombe Field'. Alternatively, the only remaining possibility is that Street persuaded Hawarden, in the early to mid 1790s, to be allowed to open up quarries on the part of Green Down that abuts Bradford Road. Such reasoning is based on the fact that the quarries at or near the top of Entry Hill do not appear to have expanded greatly after the 1787 Turnpike Map was drawn, nor do they appear in Master's 1796 'measurement' of quarries. Perhaps more significantly, by 1810, Henry Street was destined to have the greatest share of the quarries on Quarr Down, and by the time the tithes for Lyncombe and Widcombe were surveyed in 1839 it becomes clear that he was also, by then, the owner of the adjoining two acre strip between Down Field and Late Collibees known as Great Barn Ground (though the precise date of this purchase is not known).

Placed in the context of these times, the breakout of war with France in 1793 had caused economic turmoil in England resulting in, amongst other casualties, the collapse of the Bath Bank. This in turn led to the cancellation of a number of building projects, with ramifications felt all the way down the chain of builders' suppliers (Pound, 1986; 55). It is highly likely that a handful of smaller quarries were also forced to cease operations. On the other hand, a number of other projects dreamed up by individuals who continued fantasizing regardless of recession went ahead. Beckford's monumental but ultimately disastrous Fonthill Abbey scheme is a case in point. If builders, masons and quarrymen could get involved in such schemes their security would be assured. Perhaps that is what happened to Henry Street, even to the extent that he and other local quarrymen did indeed get involved with Beckford, or at least his architect James Wyatt. What is beyond dispute is that by 1806 Jeffrey Wyatt (nephew of James, and apprenticed to him until 1799) had sufficient knowledge of, and confidence in, the 26 year old Philip Nowell to appoint him master mason at the major works to be undertaken at Longleat for the Marquess of Bath. Philip was a contemporary of Henry Street Junior, and their fathers, Samuel and Henry Senior, appear to have been firm friends as well as co-'founders' of LW Byfield. This was at a time, of course, when the Wyatt family were themselves establishing a reputation as being the busiest, if not the pre-eminent architects to the wealthiest dreamers in the land.

By 1799 various quarrymen from 'Comb Down' were almost certainly considering, and more likely actually quarrying the south-eastern part of Late Collibees, or Quarr Down, next to the Ralph Allen Yard entrance to the Byfield Mine. Even though this area fell under the jurisdiction of the overseers of collection of the Poor Rates for Lyncombe and Widcombe parish, such officers were notoriously slow in updating their records, and new activities could well go unreported for months, if not a year or two. Underground quarrying would almost certainly be an activity with the capacity to fool or deceive an, appropriately named, overseer. At the northern, more visible end of Quarr Down, adjacent to the Bradford Turnpike, Henry Street may well have begun quarrying on a modest scale in 1796, or perhaps even earlier. Most likely his quarry was at the north-western corner of the two acre piece of land adjacent to Down Field, just to the west of the place where the Foresters public house now stands. This, it is suggested, was the site of the principal quarrying activity engaged in by Street and referred to in the Rate Books during the last years of the 18th century.

The fact that this area *was* quarried around this time is suggested by the Tithe Maps of 1839 (Lyncombe and Widcombe) and 1851 (Monkton Combe). This may seem a somewhat unusual statement to anyone familiar with these maps and their Apportionment Schedules. One of the great frustrations with the Combe Down Tithe Maps is that they give virtually no detail of quarrying activity because they are on lands or include premises upon which '*no rent charge has been apportioned*'. This meant, in effect, that no record was made of the owners, occupiers, or land use of these plots. However, it seems it was precisely because these lands were 'historic' quarries that they were exempted from paying church tithes. (Four, more recent quarries situated on the north side of Bradford Road did not share this advantage and *were* subject to assessment and tithe charges in 1851.) More importantly, a careful look at the distribution of areas exempted suggests that only surface quarries were included, and that areas overlying *underground* quarries *were* assessed (fig. 6). Of course the surface plot boundaries do not coincide precisely with the extent of underground workings, but the general patterns established over the whole area of Combe Down stone extraction are remarkably similar and also correlate well with the results of recent bore-hole surveys. The area in question (plot 513 on the LW Tithe Map) is clearly shown by this reasoning to be an 'historic' surface quarry. The only conclusion to be drawn from this reasoning is that this site, quarried by Henry Street, is the best candidate for the elusive Widcombe Field Quarry. If these suppositions are true, by 1800 LW Byfield was just beginning to be exploited from two fronts – one, a resumption of quarrying in the immediate vicinity of the King William IV pub (part of the '*Coomb Down Quarry*' identified in Master's 1796 survey), and the other a relatively new quarry in the immediate vicinity of the Foresters pub ('*Widcombe Field Quarry*').

The Quarr Down Purchase

In 1802, a few months before the death of Lord Hawarden, 'Late Collibees Green Down, or Quarr Down' was purchased by Harry Salmon, '*Gent of the City of Bath*'. Salmon was a speculator in land and perhaps, in modern terminology, could have been better described as a property developer. Various gleanings from the Rate Books, newspaper notices, and private deeds of sale from the first decade of the 19th century show him, for example, to have interests and dealings at the masons' yards at Dolemeads (the area of river and canal wharves at Widcombe), and to have occupied property at the prestigious new suburban development called Devonshire Buildings, just off the Wells Road near Bear Flat. Invariably he appears to have been in close contact with the quarrymasters and masons of Combe Down, and his purchase of Quarr Down was almost certainly undertaken in collusion with these men to facilitate the expansion of quarrying into Lyncombe and Widcombe parish.

Of the twenty or so acres of 'Late Collibees' shown on the 1799 Bruton map, the southernmost portion of approximately 5 acres was sold on immediately to Mr. Mighill, a farmer of Horsecombe Vale. The remainder of the land, containing the outcrops of Combe Down limestone (part of the Greater Oolite), was divided into a further two portions. These were separated by a road, 12 feet in width, '*to be built at Mr. Salmons' expense*', running perpendicular from Combe Road to the western edge of Quarr Down. Only a short section of the road was ever constructed, but this can still be seen as a trackway between No's 32 and 34 Combe Road. The sole purpose of this road was to facilitate removal of cut stone, and a second new road, for the same purpose, was intended to be built as an extension of Combe Road to follow the parish boundary southwards in the vicinity of present Rock Hall Lane.

The southernmost portion of land was effectively delineated by these 'intended' roads and is recognised today as the area of land above, below, and behind the King William IV pub. Fortunately, deeds for the sale of this property (in August, 1805) have survived, and these include wonderful 'margin maps' which illustrate extremely well how Salmon divided Quarr Down for sale to individual quarrymasters (Bath City

Archives, MH/7/14). First, the land was divided into three equal portions of precisely 2 acres and 35 perches each (fig. 7). For the greater part these portions consisted of parallel rectangular strips running along the east-west axis. This uniformity of shape was interrupted, however, by the crescent-shaped enclosure referred to earlier which appears to have been the original extension of quarry into Lyncombe and Widcombe, adjacent to the entrance to the Byfield Mine at Ralph Allen's Yard. This area coincides with, in terms of the modern landscape, the south-western half of Ralph Allen's Yard, Rock Hall Cottages, the lower portion of Rock Hall Lane, much of Rock Hall itself, and the King William IV pub car park. Here, the plot boundaries 'fanned out' from a pivotal point on the parish boundary (presently an unmarked spot situated just behind Rock Hall Cottages) to various points along the presumed quarry face from whence the rectangular strips commence. The rectangular strips contained the area of unquarried stone. The triangular fan-shaped strips adjacent to the parish boundary, along which the lines for an intended 30 feet wide road are also drawn, ensured that all the quarrymasters had equal and uninterrupted access to and from their quarry workings. This meant the potential inconvenience (and cost) of having to convey stone over a neighbour's property (known as 'wayleave') was avoided. Today, the boundary wall of one of the fan-shaped sections can still be seen. It is the wall running along the back of the car park at the King William IV pub.

The nature and timing of the deal between Harry Salmon and the three quarrymasters who were to occupy these plots- Samuel Nowell, William Hulonce, and Jonathan Rudman - is of interest. It was agreed that Nowell would have the southernmost plot and Hulonce the northernmost. The central plot was to be held in trust by them as *'tenants in common'*, and then leased to Jonathan Rudman for a yearly rent of £20 subject to the provision that Rudman could *"...purchase a further interest in the same land so leased ..."* (Ibid.). This suggests that Rudman could not initially afford his share of the total purchase price of just over £726 and that his neighbours covered him by splitting the total cost between them until such time as Rudman could pay his full share. This appears to have occurred within a few months of the sale in August, 1805, since all subsequent records suggest Rudman owned his own land. In fact all three had already commenced quarrying this area at least one year before, according to the Rate Books held at Bath City Archives (Sept. 1804), and all three appear also in the quarry extraction records of the Harwarden Estates, 1795-98 (Pollard, 1994, 11). The strong possibility exists that it is they who had been responsible for quarrying this part of Lyncombe and Widcombe in the first place or, more likely, had re-opened this section of quarry after it was abandoned about the time of Ralph Allen's death. A degree of friendly rivalry no doubt existed between these men since they operated independently, but this and plenty of other evidence suggests they were always prepared, if possible, to help each other out in times of difficulty. The problem of finding sufficient funds to pay the purchase price may also explain why this section of Quarr Down was sold as much as two years later than the northern half.

It is unfortunate that the original deed of sale for the northern half of Quarr Down remains undiscovered. The information that follows has had to be derived from subsequent deeds of sale, most of which are in private possession, and which refer only to portions of the total land area. What seems clear, however, is that Salmon made a similar partition of land into three (presumably) equal plots of rectangular shape. In contrast to the southern half they were aligned north-south rather than east-west, and also somewhat smaller in area than the southern plots. They were sold in 1803 to Henry Street (westernmost plot), John Scrace (the easternmost plot - adjoining Combe Road), and Abraham Sumsion (central plot). These three names appear together with Nowell, Hulonce, and Rudman as quarrymasters, for the first time, in the September 1804 Rate Books for the Parish of Lyncombe and Widcombe. These six men are the true founders of the LW Byfield 'Mine'. Meanwhile, two other names require a mention with regard to MC Byfield. These are Richard and James Lankesheer, who quarried (underground) the old Allen workings from the mine entrances at Ralph Allen's Yard, in Monkton Combe Parish. Their rights to quarry were confirmed in a separate deal with the Hadley family, dated 1809, on land "...*bounded on the southwest by a strip of land ... some time since allotted for the purpose of a road*". This was of course the road intended to be shared with the immediate neighbours of the Lankesheers - Nowell, Hulonce, and Rudman - for the sake of transporting quarried stone (Bath City Archives, MH/7/17).

The Byfield Landscape: 1805

It is useful at this stage to embark on a flight of fancy and take a bird's-eye view of the landscape as it might have appeared on October 21st, 1805, not long after Harry Salmon had successfully concluded his dealings with his friends - the quarrymasters there. Perhaps he is celebrating in a Bath coffee-house, or ruminating over the latest news sheet. Far away the Battle of Trafalgar rages.

The bird is flying north over an area of downland, steep sided but with a gently sloping crest. Away to the right, above the southern slopes of the down, the nascent village of Combe Down is emerging. There is a row of weather-beaten cottages next to a grander looking terrace, three stories high. Below these, the landscape is badly scarred where stone has been torn from the land. Men are labouring to hide this slash by carting barrow loads of dirt to cover it. The newly carpeted terrace will allow cultivation of food. Foundations are also being strengthened for a new row of cottages - the first of which is having its roof timbers covered with slate. The names given to these places, now or at a later time, are de Montalt Place, Isabella Place, and Quarryvale. On the Down, here and there, the landscape is similarly slashed and scarred. A quarry just behind Isabella Place possibly has a man by the name of Davidge working there. A cottage or two is being built here too. Squared blocks of stone are stored alongside. In the midst of all this a gaping hole leads underground - the focus of slow but steadfast endeavour. On the land between there is more activity as men chop and saw at fir trees. Tree stumps cover much of this barren landscape.

Rutted cart tracks wend through the old fir plantations - one of them to the mine entrance directly below. Here the Lankesheers are working. Much later this place will be known as Byfield, then Gammon's Yard, then Ralph Allen's Yard. A little to the left the thin surface soil and vegetation are being stripped away to reveal a honey-yellow rock outcrop. Sam Nowell and his men literally pick their way over it, hewing great blocks of stone and gently lowering them away. There is a similar scene nearby, where Jonathan Rudman and his crew work the side of the outcrop, just around the corner from Nowell. From here the outcrop disappears into the gently rising slope of the Down. Will Hulonce and his men work with pick, saw, and shovels, as they excavate an incline into the hillside as if to burrow after the stone. Further on, next to the turnpike road which follows the crest of the Down, John Scrace and his workers are doing the same thing - only they are digging towards William Hulonce. At this rate it looks as if they will meet up someday, somewhere deep underground. A bigger scar cuts the hillside a little over to the west. Henry Street is well established here - but he's no tunneller. Although painfully slow he has opted to strip away the 'brash' and other rubbish rocks from the surface in order to get to the honeyed freestone below. Most of his workers have to load all this detritus onto barrows to haul away elsewhere along a network of plank walkways; this before they can even begin to quarry the more valuable stone. All these quarries are relatively new - except for the old Allen workings of course - and there is not yet any sign of permanent housing. Only a few wooden shacks have been set up for the other masters and workers at the places where they work. The bird flies on by.

Illustrations

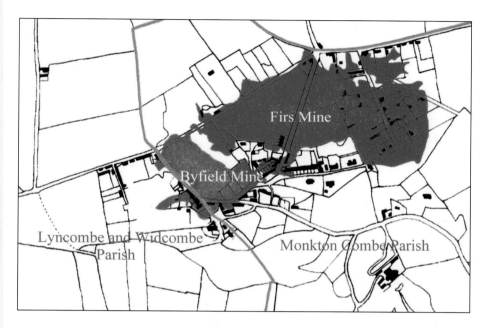

Figure 1. A map showing the locations of the Byfield and Firs Mines, and the boundary between Monkton Combe and Lyncombe and Widcombe Parishes (blue line). The 'Mines' represent only the areas of underground quarrying activity, as determined by recent survey work. They adjoined substantial areas of surface quarry, particularly to the south and west of the undermined area (see Fig. 6). The village map is a composite of the Tithe Commutation Award Maps drawn for both parishes between 1839 and 1851. This is the period just after the years when large scale and widespread quarrying activity in Combe Down came to an end.

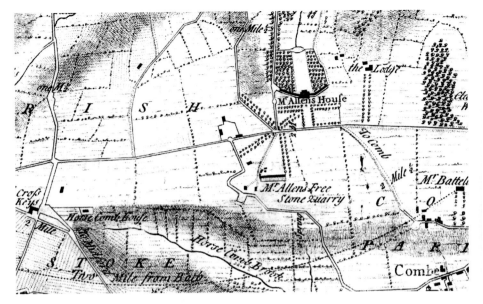

Figure 2. A detail from Thomas Thorpe's 'Survey of Five Miles Around Bath', dated 1742, highlighting *Mr Allens Free Stone Quarry*. The three buildings shown to the left of Allen's row of cottages are crane houses, suggesting three sites of quarry activity. The large open 'square' adjoining the road to Combe village is the site of Byfield Place, a later construction, and the area now referred to as Ralph Allen's Yard.

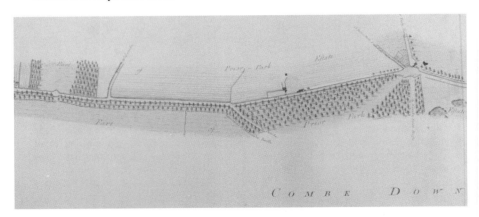

Figure 3. A detail from Charles Master's 'Survey of Bath's Turnpike Roads', dated 1787. This strip map of land lying immediately adjacent to the Bradford Turnpike Road highlights the extent to which Allen's fir plantations had expanded and matured, compared to those shown in Thorpe's map of 1742. This comparison also demonstrates how Allen moved the road 'To Combe' to its present location.

Figure 4. *(opposite page top)* A detail from Charlton's map of Lyncombe and Widcombe, 1799. The survey was commissioned by the Trustees of Bruton Hospital to clarify the actual extent of their properties within the parish. Details of ownership often appear to clash with claims made in the Survey of Manors Belonging to Ralph Allen (Fig. 5). This detail shows the location of Quarr Down and the likely site of Widcombe Field Quarry. 'Hp' indicates land owned by Lord Hawarden.

Figure 5. A detail from the 'Survey of the Manours of Hampton, Claverton with Widcombe belonging to Ralph Allen Esqr.'. Although Thomas Thorpe was said to have made the survey originally, in 1741, much of the detail on the map is more consistent with the Combe Down landscape after Allen's death in 1764. The representation of trees in the crescent-shaped area to the south of Combe Road appears to be a later addition to the original map. Ralph Allen's Yard is located at the bottom tip of this crescent, straddling the parish boundary (shown as a red line extending from Combe Road to the bottom of the map).

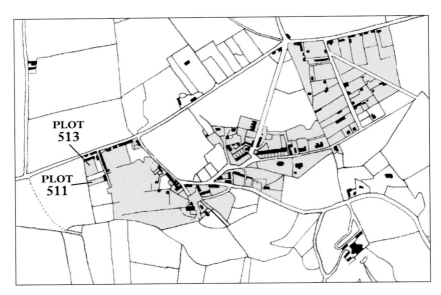

Figure 6. A composite map showing property boundaries as drawn on the 1839 LW Tithe Map and the 1851 MC Tithe Map. The shaded area indicates areas which were exempt from paying church tithes because they were 'historic' surface quarries. Land overlying underground quarries was subject to tithe charges. Plot 513 is the likely site of Widcombe Field Quarry, opened by Henry Street in the 1790s.

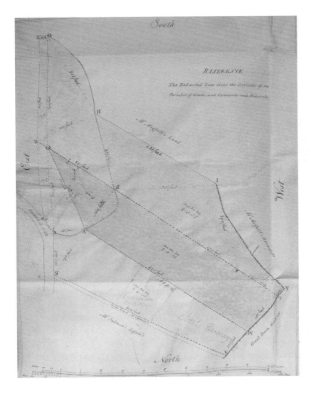

Figure 7. Deed of sale 'margin map' illustrating how Harry Salmon divided up the southern portion of unquarried land in LW Byfield for sale in August, 1805. The quarrymasters who purchased were Samuel Nowell (pink), Jonathan Rudman (green), and William Hulonce (yellow). The fan or crescent-shaped section can be compared to the same area as represented on the 1799 Charlton (Bruton) map (fig 4.), and on the Survey of the Manors of Ralph Allen (fig 5.)

Figure 8. An engraving by J. Hassall of 'Free Stone Quarries', near Bath, drawn in 1791. The view is romanticised, and the exact location is not certain. The overall impression, however, suggests how the surface workings near Ralph Allen's Yard may have appeared at the turn of the 18th century. *(Reproduced by courtesy of the Victoria Art Gallery, Bath).*

Figures 9a and 9b. Photographs of the incline excavated by William Hulonce to access his area of underground quarry workings. Fig.9a shows the surface entrance looking down the incline, located behind Tor View. Subsequent modifications, including the replacement of surface topsoil after initial workings ceased; the building of steps to allow access to the mine for use as an air-raid shelter; and the erection of a grill to prevent unlawful access to the dangerous mines make interpretation difficult. Fig. 9b is a view looking up the incline taken shortly after the area had been cleared of accumulated debris. It is the best image we get of how Hulonce's original 'works entrance' may have appeared. *(Reproduced by kind permission of Paul Deakin, FRPS).*

Figure 10. Brunswick Place, Combe Road. This was the substantial cottage William Hulonce (either Junior – probably, or Junior and Senior together – possibly) built over their former mine workings in the early 1820s.

Figure 11. The underground passageway leading from Ralph Allen's Yard to William Hulonce's workings. This was probably opened up by Hulonce in, or shortly after, 1806 and connects after a short distance with the inclined entrance behind Tor View, also opened by him (Fig. 9). The circular structure is the '*well*' referred to by Hulonce when he granted Henry Street Jnr. the right to use this entrance in 1813. It is situated under the 'yard' entrance to the King William IV pub, and was probably used as a source of water when the Combe Down Brewery was established here in the late 1850s. (*Reproduced by kind permission of Paul Deakin, FRPS*).

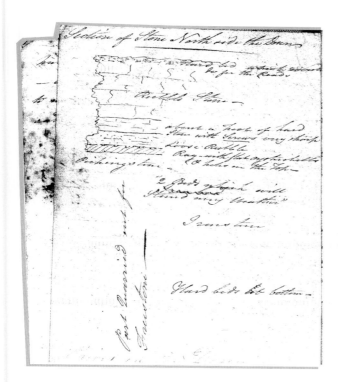

Figure 12. A page from William Smith's notebook showing a 'Section of Stone' on the 'Northside the Down'. The sketch, drawn on a visit to the Combe Down quarries in 1811, highlights the considerable depth of 'ridding' that overlay the freestone at this site.

Figure 13. Deed of Sale 'margin map' showing the former quarry land, subsequently infilled, which was bought for the purposes of creating a Jewish Burial Ground, in 1812. It is likely that William Smith drew his sketch of 'A Section of Stone' (fig. 12) somewhere on this site.

Figure 14. The King William IV pub, from its front, south facing aspect, more or less as constructed in the mid 1820s. Rock Hall Lane is to the right of the picture, leading up to Combe Road. Ralph Allen's Yard is further to the right. A rough pencil sketch of this site can be seen in Fig. 7, drawn when the Lane was first conceived of to provide equal and practical access to the quarries here.

Figure 15. Rock Hall, as photographed in the 1930s. The building on the left is the original Rock Hall Cottage, built by Samuel Nowell around 1810 and later the home of his son, also called Samuel. Another son, named Philip, gained fame and fortune by working as stone mason on some of the most prestigious building projects in England during the first decades of the 19th century. He built the Gothic-looking structure on the right around 1830, after he had taken over control of the family quarry. Philip Nowell eventually died at Rock Hall in 1853.

The Byfield Quarrymasters II

The history of the Byfield Mine in the early years of the 19th century can be traced by piecing together the various tid-bits that offer clues to the lives of the Byfield quarrymasters. The evidence is scattered widely, but the following is an attempt to collate all that can be found out about these characters and to put some 'flesh' on them.

Samuel Nowell was born in 1744, somewhere in the area between Colerne and Box, in Wiltshire. Even today the broad crescent which extends from here to Melksham is where the majority of "Nowell" surnames are concentrated. His name appears frequently in the records, although variations on the spelling are also numerous. Noell, Noal, Knowel, and so on, all refer to this man or his immediate family. He married Ann Shellard of Slaughterford in 1770, and eight of their nine children are entered in the Monkton Combe baptismal register. In fact Samuel was already resident at Monkton Combe at the time of his marriage, aged 26, suggesting that he had been apprenticed here to learn the trade of stone mason (Wiltshire and Swindon Record Office, Biddestone Parish Registers). Unfortunately, registers are missing for the period 1699-1771, and the details of birth of possibly one child, possibly more, are lost. The first recorded child is Benjamin, baptized on October 25th, 1772, followed by Samuel, Ann, Phillip (sic), Jacob, Sarah, Joseph, and William - baptized June 13th, 1793.

It is conceivable that Sam Nowell served his stone mason's apprenticeship with one of the quarrymen who worked directly under Ralph Allen. Then, after settling down to a family life, he staked claim to his own section of quarry face here. His name appears on the list of rent paying quarrymasters on Viscount Hawarden estates, 1795-1798 (Pollard, op.cit.), and for the later part of this period he is recorded as receiving payment for his role as *'supervisor of quarries'* (Somerset CRO DD/X/LA 12). He was clearly a trusted figure and, it can be assumed, maintained a position of some authority. One surviving document is an Indenture of Apprenticeship for a *'poor Child'*, aged 8 years, to be taken on by Samuel for tuition and instruction in the *'business of a stone mason'* (Bath City Archives, PP729).

As a mason, and in common with all other quarrymasters at Combe Down, the primary concern of Samuel Nowell was to secure the contract to build a building. This could be a public works contract such as the Guildhall in Bath. The names Lancashire [sic], Street, and Sumsion, for example, all appear in the accounts for building the new "Town Hall & Markets", 1775 – 1778. It could also have been to construct all, or part of, a house for the nobility, such as the edifice Beckford aspired to create. Whatever, the role of the mason was first to acquire appropriate stone from the quarries, then to shape it and transport the rough blocks to the building site, then to supervise the final dressing of the stone and its incorporation into the building structure. Although credit for the final construction invariably went to the architect rather than the mason/builder, a mason such as Nowell would be likely to spend as much time as possible at the building site. This, after all, was where the fruits of all his labours would be seen and evaluated.

In the early 1790s Bath witnessed a new form of urban development - the suburban terrace. Devonshire Buildings, completed sometime between 1796 and 1798, are located at the foot of Entry Hill, but still offered a fine view of Bath from the southern slopes of the city. The first residents were the emerging 'upper middle class' including, for example, Harry Salmon. Indeed, he may have been 'the developer', the land itself having originally belonged to Collibee's estate and then earmarked for this residential project as early as 1787 according to Masters' survey of the Bath turnpikes (Somerset CRO D/T/Ba/24). Building may have been delayed as a result of the bank collapse following the outbreak of hostilities with France in 1793. Nonetheless, the Lyncombe and Widcombe Rate Books, which survive in an unbroken series from February 1796, list Devonshire Buildings initially in a separate section to the main volumes, confirming the newness of the development. Occupation of the properties within this terrace begun as soon as each individual property was completed; and amongst the other early owner/occupants is Samuel Nowell. This suggests Nowell was the principal mason on site, and that during construction he occupied part of the structure he was actually building. The rate books also suggest that he maintained ownership of property within the buildings for a few years after completion, though he was no longer resident there. Presumably this was part of his 'payment', though it could also suggest a form of partnership existed between developer, architect and builder. If so, this confirms his already strong connections with Salmon before the Quarr Down purchase in 1805.

This latter point is important, since it is clear that Nowell obtained the best deal of all the quarry masters. Although Nowell seems to have paid the same price as Hulonce and Rudman for his share of quarry, he acquired the main outcrop where the stone was exposed and, presumably, easiest to extract. His stone would therefore be cheaper than that quarried elsewhere since he would not have to go to the considerable expense of mining, or of removing a substantial overburden of valueless brash and rubble. One can easily imagine Nowell's quarry being similar in appearance to Hassall's print of 'Free Stone Quarries near Bath' drawn in 1791 and now displayed in the Victoria Art Galleries, Bath (fig. 8).

In the few years after 1805 Nowell may have maintained property in Monkton Combe, or he may have lived wherever his next building project had taken him, or, he may have built some crude accommodation next to his quarry. By 1810, however, he had constructed a more substantial home for himself and his family for he was now charged rates for a house at the site of the quarry. The cottage was built on the first part to be worked out, nearest the road by the parish boundary, on the site now occupied by Rock Hall. Evidence that this did indeed become the Nowell family home is clear in his will, dated 1815, although it is also apparent that by this time a second cottage had been constructed to accommodate some of his younger sons and their families (Bath City Archives, PP729). This is likely to have been the lower of the Rock Hall Cottages (No. 6). Samuel was succeeded by his second son, also named Samuel, when he died in 1816 aged 72. His obituary in the Bath Chronicle called him a '*quarrymaster*', though another of his sons, Philip, was later to describe him as a '*builder*' on the occasion of Philip's second marriage in 1850 (Bath City Archives, Lyncombe and Widcombe Parish Registers). By trade he was a 'stone mason' and it was in this role that he was qualified to take on apprentices. His sons also would have served an apprenticeship, possibly under his own tutelage but more likely elsewhere. In fact Philip, the third son, was to become so successful as a stone mason that he would eventually bring fame and fortune to the family.

The 'intended road' between the Lyncombe and Widcombe and the Monkton Combe parish boundaries was never constructed exactly as had been planned. Immediately after the purchase by Nowell, Rudman, and Hulonce of their shares of Quarr Down they seem to have agreed that a more sensible option was for the road to veer towards the existing quarry face. All three agreed to share equal and uninterrupted access to their own section of quarry (Bath City Archives, MH/7/14). This road is the line now followed by Rock Hall Lane. In terms of the modern landscape, the road to

Rock Hall accessed Nowell's quarry, the driveway to Tor View was Rudman's access to his quarry, and the area of the King William IV pub car park gave entry to Hulonce's workings. This arrangement caused potential difficulty for the Lankesheers, who were now 'cut off' on the other side of the parish boundary. The expedient solution was for a series of small land swaps with the Lankesheers, allowing them direct access to the new road. Certainly Nowell and Hulonce were involved in this exchange, soon after the initial land purchase in 1805 (Bath City Archives, MH/7/14, MH/7/9, and others). The land in question almost certainly included the south-western corner of Ralph Allen's Yard, though precise identification of the plots is extremely difficult.

The **Lankesheers**, James and Richard, are most commonly associated with the village of Widcombe though their family name remained inextricably linked with quarrying at Combe Down until at least the middle of the 19th century (Population Census, 1851). According to the Viscount Hawarden rent records for stone extraction they were by far and away the most productive family on the Down during the 1790s (Pollard, 1994). They were most likely father and son, and Widcombe baptismal records suggest James' eldest son, also named James, became a plumber whilst his younger brother, Richard, learned the craft of the stone mason (Bath City Archives). Thereafter, the profession of quarrymaster/stone mason passed down the line of Richard Lankesheer, through other Richards.

Given the Lankesheers known association with the Byfield Mine entrance at Ralph Allen's Yard it can be said with virtual certainty that they quarried the original Allen workings at this site, presumably pushing the face ever further to the north and north-east. James could well have been born within Ralph Allen's lifetime, but given that he appears in a trade directory entry for 1819 it seems unlikely he ever worked under Allen. Perhaps, though, *his* father had done so. The Hawarden rent records suggest that Richard Lankesheer took over a quarry face previously worked by Richard Singers. In a private communication David Pollard recalled that when, on one occasion, he mentioned these names at a public lecture someone in the audience claimed Richard Singers to be his ancestor, and that family tradition declared Singers *had* been a quarryman once employed by Allen. If true, this is perhaps the only case where continuity can be traced from Allen's day to the early 19th century. It is possible that Richard Lankesheer had been apprenticed to Singers and 'inherited' his section of quarry on Singers death or retirement in 1796. Alternatively he simply bought the rights to the vacant plot. Whatever, the Lankesheers now became the dominant stone producers on Combe Down according to the rent records.

Despite their dominance, the annual sequence of the rent records, covering the years 1795 – 1799, indicates that the Lankesheer's stone output declined steadily over this period. This is also true in the case of two other quarrymasters, Robert Simpkin and Peter Cromwell, whose location in the records suggest they also worked underground in MC Byfield (Somerset CRO DD/X/LA 12). This may just be a reflection of a worsening economic environment at this time. Indeed, most quarrymasters named in the record showed some decline in output. On the other hand it could indicate a dwindling supply of stone in the old underground quarries, and point to the fact that stone extraction from MC Byfield was entering its final phase. This would have rekindled a desire for the westward expansion of quarrying across the parish boundary, and may also have been a factor in the opening of Widcombe Field Quarry at this time.

Returning to the Lankesheers, Richard Lankesheer is the name which most frequently appears on deeds relating to the quarry after 1805 although the 1819 Bath Trades Directory lists both Richard and James. The entries are intriguing, for they suggest that underground quarrying at this site may have, by then, come to an end for them. James had by this time assumed the role of *'conveyancer'*, with offices in St James Parade, Bath. He had also been appointed *'commissioner for taking special bail'*, with offices at Prospect Place, Combe Down. Quite what this means is unclear, although in the context of the times - the middle of an economic recession following Waterloo and the end of the Napoleonic Wars - the possibility of bankruptcy among quarrymasters was very real and the threat of debtors prison (in London) ever present. The address – 'Prospect Place' - seems to place him at Byfield Mine. Even today a cottage by that name exists just above the old entrance to the mine, part of a larger structure now incorporating the Bath Crockhire Company. It is very possible that this property was built by the Lankesheers around 1810, since it is within the bounds of the land sold to them by Hadley in 1809 (Bath City Archives, MH/7/17).

The property was probably intended for use by Richard, but the 1819 Directory suggests he was at that time living in Widcombe as a 'stone mason'. Parish Registers from this period confirm the continued presence of members of the Lankesheer (also spelt Lancashire) family in Widcombe - in Waterloo Buildings and in Caroline Buildings – names most certainly evocative of the age and thus suggestive of the fact they had been newly constructed or were in the process of being built. The Lankesheers did maintain connections with quarrying at Combe Down, but their name no longer appears in association with this part of Byfield Mine. In 1851 the

Monkton Combe Tithe Map, for example, shows that a Richard Lankesheer was engaged in an entirely separate quarry north of North Road (Bath City Archives).

The mine entrance in Ralph Allen's Yard was still being used in 1819, but it seems the direction of quarrying activity was shifting away from the old Allen workings (MC Byfield) towards Hulonce's quarry, in Lyncombe and Widcombe. Of interest is the fact that some new cottages had just been built, called Byfield Buildings. As Pollard has noted: "A visitor wrote in 1819: *'Byfield Buildings is … pleasantly situated and a few paces forwards, the visitor, if inclinations permit him, may descend into the stone quarries at Combe Down open[ed] and worked by Mr. Allen.'*" (Pollard, 1994, 14). The buildings had been named after James Byfield, who occupied one of them. (His widow Mariah, aged 55 years, was still an occupant there in 1841 according to the Population Census.) James Byfield was a *'haullier'* at this time, almost certainly transporting stone from the quarries to various destinations in Bath, or to the canal wharves at Dolemeads and at Dundas. This is the man after whom the Byfield Mine is named and, within a few years, he indeed became a quarrymaster in his own right. He will re-appear a little later in this narrative but, for the moment, it is worth noting the dangers associated with hauling stone. The following item appeared in the Bath Chronicle on 9th September, 1819:

Robert Byfield in driving his brothers waggon into a Quarry on Combe Down, the horses turned suddenly and upset the waggon upon him, by which his back was so dreadfully injured that he died last night at the Casualty Hospital, where he was taken immediately after the accident.

Immediately adjacent to the Ralph Allen's Yard mine entrance, on the other side of the parish boundary, was the quarry belonging to **Jonathan Rudman**. He appears on the list of Viscount Hawarden's quarry rentals, but is one of the least productive quarrymasters recorded there. Between 1795 and 1798 he quarried less than half the amount of stone extracted by William Hulonce and only one quarter the amount taken by Samuel Nowell. This could help explain why, in 1805, he appears to have been struggling to find cash. Unfortunately, as yet, virtually nothing is known about his background, place of origin, or even workplace. What is known is that in the April, 1807 Parish Rate Book the word 'late' is penciled alongside Rudman's name. He died young, probably in his mid thirties, as far as information can be gleaned from parish registers and the Population Census. His son, named John, was aged only ten or eleven, and may already have commenced an apprenticeship in the 'business of stone mason' with one of his neighbours - possibly Henry Street. The remarkable thing is that, with the help and apparent encouragement of these very same neighbours, the Rudmans were able to continue operating and, in the final outcome, eventually prove to be one of the most enduring of the Byfield quarrymaster families

The credit for all this must go to Jonathan's wife, Sophia. In the years between Trafalgar and Waterloo it was not so uncommon that women were forced to seek a means of making an independent living. To take on the role of quarrymaster, however, in a profession not just dominated by men but within and into which women were barely even seen, much less admitted, seems truly formidable. Parallels with Masonic Lodges come readily to mind - given that mastery of a quarry and its activity lay near the very heart of the mason's profession. Sophia was to be the dominant force in the Rudman quarry until her death around 1833 (Bath City Archives, Parish Rate Books).

The transition of ownership from Jonathan to Sophia seems to have gone smoothly at first, and doubtless kind neighbours played a crucial role in this. For the first four or five years after his death everything is recorded as normal in the Rate Books, with Mrs. Rudman being charged exactly the same rate as all other Byfield quarrymasters (6 shillings per quarry). In common with most of her neighbours she claimed an exemption from payment due to poverty - perhaps justly so. Her home was probably a wooden shack - a 'temporary structure' exempted from additional rate charges. By 1810, however, other quarrymasters were constructing permanent stone cottages (Nowell and Lankesheer, for example) but she apparently lacked the means and wherewithal to follow this trend. In 1812 Sophia and her children occupied a rateable albeit small structure; owned by Mr. Lankershere (sic). A year later Henry Street (probably Jnr.) had taken over ownership of the cottage, and Sophia paid rent to him for the next four years. In 1817 the Rate Books show that Mrs. Rudman was chargeable both for her own quarry as well as her own 'house'. There is evidence to suggest that Henry Street Jnr. worked closely with the Lankesheers (he might well have been apprenticed to Richard), and that he was involved in the underground workings in the vicinity of Sector X (Bath City Archives, MH/7/14). He was twenty years older than young John Rudman, but may have acted as mentor to him. It seems quite reasonable to suggest that the properties owned by Lankesheer, then Street, were one and the same, and that in 1817 it became Sophia Rudman's own cottage. John Rudman may even have assisted in building it. In 1817 John reached the age of 21, and returned to the Rudman quarry to help his mother. Perhaps the cottage was a form of coming-of-age present, especially so if it had been built on Rudman land. But this is mere speculation. What is clear is that Sophia Rudman was still quarrymaster.

In 1820, after years of economic recession, the Rudmans disappear from the Rate Books for a while. These were bad years for almost all the quarrymasters in Combe Down, and Sophia Rudman was by no means alone in being sued for debt at this time. In fact the Bath Chronicle reports she had been declared bankrupt in 1819, describing her, perhaps rather contemptuously, as '*a quarrywoman, dealer, and chapwoman*' (Bath Chronicle, 7th October, 1819). The exact outcome of these proceedings is not known, but in 1825, when the Rate Books were rearranged in order of place rather than surname, Sophia Rudman reappears as quarrymaster. In the same year she was again the subject of a newspaper report. This time one of her workers is reported to have been killed when he fell from a plank walkway crossing above the quarry while pushing a barrow. The scene is highly reminiscent of Beazer's description (and accompanying photograph) of quarry working on Combe Down in the 1930s (Beazer, 1981, 85), and is strongly indicative of the fact that the Rudmans worked their quarries above rather than below ground. The judge at the inquest of the unfortunate quarryman is reported to have admonished Sophia for her disregard of the dangers of the working practices then employed in the quarries, and advised her to find '*wider planks*' (Bath Chronicle, 25th May, 1825).

The cottage occupied by the Rudmans abutted the northern boundary of their quarry ground, near the eastern end. In this sense it mirrors almost exactly the location of Samuel Nowell's house, and confirms that the direction of quarrying was generally from east to west. In other words, permanent housing was constructed on ground which had first been, and was the first to have been quarried and, if required, backfilled. The Rudman cottage was eventually remodelled in the early 1860s to become the villa still known as Tor View. In the garden behind Tor View, on part of the land that was sold by Harry Salmon to William Hulonce, is an inclined entrance to the underground section of LW Byfield. Almost certainly this section was opened up by Hulonce himself, perhaps as he worked alongside Rudman in exposing this section of the Oolitic outcrop. Both would have benefited by clearing a platform on top of the freestone by removing the 'brash' and rubble (or 'ridding') along their mutual boundary. Rudman, working to the south and west had a thinner overlying cover of brash and so preferred open quarrying. Hulonce, heading north from this point, chose this location to tunnel down into the freestone, and so follow Ralph Allen's example by opening a new mine (fig. 9a and 9b).

One of the problems concerning research into this era of quarrymasters is that father and first-born son invariably share the same name. Jonathan Rudman, Henry Street, Samuel Nowell (with his second son) and, probably, the Lankesheers all followed this tradition. So too did **William Hulonce**, but in this case distinguishing the 'Elder' and the 'Younger' seems particularly difficult. William the Elder is celebrated for building much of Bathwick in the last years of the 18th century. He paid rental to Viscount Hawarden for quarrying at this time and was likely to have been instrumental in developing 'Quarr Down' in Lyncombe and Widcombe parish. The 1819 Trade Directory describes the Elder as a '*quarryman*', with an address at Cottage Row on Bathwick Street. Conversely, '*Jnr.*' is described as a '*stone mason*', residing at Combe Down. Logic would suggest that a quarryman (master) should live nearer the quarries and that a mason should be near the site of building construction! Rate Books suggest that the connection between William Hulonce and the Byfield Mine continued (albeit intermittently) until the end of the 1830s, possibly 1840. This suggests it was indeed William the Younger who maintained residential links with Combe Down. Crucially, a letter from a creditor dated 1836 and addressed to Robert Clark, a tenant of Hulonce living on Combe Road, refers to '*William Hulonce late of Bathwick*' (Bath City Archives, MH/7/14). The letter advises Clark not to pay rent to William the Younger since the author, James Gooden, is still owed money by Hulonce and instructs that future rental payments should be made directly to him. The debt, of £300, was incurred in the period 1818-1821 by William the Elder. Beyond this knowledge it is very difficult to distinguish Elder and Younger. In the following, somewhat complicated story of the Hulonce connection with the Byfield Mine it has to be accepted that the responsibility for quarrying at Combe Down was passed from father to son at some point, possibly around 1815, but both seem to have maintained some degree of involvement until, at the latest, the mid 1830s.

The underground section of LW Byfield lies almost entirely in the plot of quarry ground purchased by Hulonce in 1805. There are three known entrances to this area (also known as Sector S) - at Ralph Allen's Yard; to the rear of Tor View (also referred to as Irvine's [sic] Incline); and at the extreme western edge of the workings (referred to commonly as the Byfield Mine Entrance) (Willies, 2002). In 1805 the Ralph Allen's Yard entrance led to the Lankesheer quarries and there is no evidence to suggest that, before that time, Hulonce had any right of entry or egress there. Rather, he demised a small portion of his land in 1806 so that Richard Lankesheer might have untroubled access to his own quarry and the right to carry stone away (Bath City Archives, MH/7/14 and MH/7/16). It is likely to have been at this time, therefore, that Hulonce cut through the 'extended pillar' which marked the parish boundary underground to provide a second underground access to his own quarry, and so create a third underground entrance in Ralph Allen's Yard.

Almost from the moment of Hulonce's purchase he resold the greater part of his property to other quarrymen. Just one day after the original purchase, on 26th August 1805, Hulonce demised the westernmost section of his plot to Patrick Byrne, a mason from Widcombe. The terms dictated that for a consideration of £200, plus an annual rent of six pence, Byrne would enjoy *the sole and exclusive liberty to quarry and dig, cut up, or carry away ... stone* from ground measured as *one statute acre*, with a line to be drawn subsequently to delineate the east facing boundary. Since Salmon's intended 12' road had not yet been completed, Byrne was also granted the right to transport his stone to Combe Road across Hulonce's property (extracted from private deeds, 'Abstract of Title, 1883'). The 'Byfield Mine Entrance' to the underground workings lies within the land demised to Byrne, near the easternmost boundary. The direction of underground working is to the east, away from Byrne's property, but underlies another plot demised by Hulonce - to Abraham Sumsion, in March 1807 (Bath City Archives, MH/7/14). It is clear, therefore, that Hulonce was not responsible for the opening of this, the westernmost entrance to the underground quarries.

The entrance behind Tor View is on land that belonged to Hulonce and which was never sold by him or leased to others. The shallow incline, which runs along a length of about 25 yards, leads to a level approximately two-thirds of the way down the depth of the freestone stratum. The direction of the tunnel is north-easterly, heading towards the rear of Brunswick Place, on Combe Road. According to the Rate Books this was the house that Hulonce (the Younger?) built for himself, in the early 1820s (fig. 10). The location of the incline is intriguing since it runs away from the most obvious routes for transportation of stone. The incline is perpendicular to the line of the natural rock outcrop, however, suggesting that Hulonce merely 'burrowed' after the stone as it disappeared into the hillside. His ambitions regarding the quarrying of stone seem in any case to have been somewhat limited, the intention perhaps being to extract no more than he required for his own building projects in Bathwick. This would help explain why he sold the quarry rights of such a large portion of his land to others. It could also reflect the possibility that quarrying underground was a more time consuming and, arguably, a more expensive process than surface quarrying.

The decision whether to open a surface quarry or to quarry underground depended on a number of factors. First, the excavation and removal of overlying brash and useless 'ridding' required a considerable amount of non-productive labour. There was also the problem of finding an appropriate facility to store this waste, since the usual terms for a quarry lease stipulated that land should be restored almost to its former height after the quarry was worked out. Then, the cost and effort of transporting all this waste material had to be considered. The 'discards' could not be merely thrown away! The main advantage of surface quarrying, on the other hand, was that large blocks of stone could be removed with relative ease once the freestone had been exposed, and that there was no wastage of freestone because there was no need to leave 'pillars' to support a roof. Most likely, for most quarrymasters, it was the overall thickness of the overlying brash which determined whether to quarry above or below ground. Of course, those quarrying underground would desire the security offered by a thicker and stronger roof. The relative thinness of the roof in many parts of Combe Down – the very problem confronted by the community today – reflects just how marginal this decision must have been in many cases.

Whatever the considerations that occupied Hulonce's thoughts, the Rate Books suggest that in 1816 he temporarily ceased quarrying. His name simply disappears from the Books, until 1822 when he is again charged rates for house and quarry. It could well be that Hulonce had actually given up quarrying earlier. In 1813 he granted to Henry Street the right to use underground passageways beneath Hulonce land, as well as access to his pump, or well. This well was a prominent underground feature in the LW Byfield Mine, being situated near the Ralph Allen's Yard entrance recently excavated by Hulonce (fig. 11). The same Memorandum suggests that Street was at this time working on the Monkton Combe side of the mine, possibly in the area of the recently rediscovered Sector X (Bath City Archives, MH/7/14). The Henry Street in question must have been the son of his like-named quarrymaster father. In fact Henry Street Senior appears to have retired from quarrying about this time. Henry Street Junior's purpose was clearly to connect with his father's quarries, which by now included the land previously sold by Hulonce to Abraham Sumsion.

Abraham Sumsion was another of the original group of quarrymasters to purchase from Harry Salmon, and held the central strip of land which extended south from Bradford Road as far as the 12 ft. 'intended roadway' half-way down Combe Road. By purchasing land and quarry rights from Hulonce he extended his holdings through the central axis of LW Byfield. This would seem appropriate for the member of a family which for so long was connected with the quarries at Combe Down. The name Sumsion (or Sumption, etc.) appears prominently in the Monkton Combe Parish records from the 1770s onwards. The 1777 accounts for the building of the new Town Hall and Markets in Bath include a payment to Isaac Sumsion for 'Free Stone'; the 1841 Population Census records that two of the six quarrymasters then operating on Combe Down (both parishes) were called Isaac Sumsion – one aged 60 and the other aged 40 years; and in 1887 when most of the surviving independent quarrymasters in the Bath, Box, and Corsham areas joined forces to form Bath Stone Firms Ltd. another Isaac Sumsion appears in the list of signatories. Isaac appears to be the favoured patriarchal name, but the parish registers are replete with Abrahams, Samuels, Sarahs, and so on. There can be little doubt that the Abraham Sumsion of LW Byfield was a close member of this notable family. The only slightly unusual feature is that Abraham was working in Lyncombe and Widcombe at all. The main base of the Sumsion operations was on the other side of the former Allen and Hawarden estates – in the area around Shaft Road and Lodge Style, where quarrying still continues today.

Abraham died in 1809 and all his land in LW Byfield was purchased by his neighbour, Henry Street Senior. It is impossible to say whether or not he actually quarried the underground workings adjacent to the Byfield Quarry Entrance, underlying the plot of land he purchased from Hulonce in 1807. Perhaps, though, his desire was simply to acquire land in order to build a house for himself. The site does indeed boast one of the oldest properties on Combe Road (No. 34), and its present name – Trafalgar Cottage – is certainly indicative of construction at this time. Also, in terms of quarrying activity, it seems more likely that Sumsion was kept busy at the northern end of his plot, next to the Bradford Road.

Recent archaeological evidence suggests a quarry face existed parallel to, and a few metres south of Bradford Road, between Combe Road and Greendown Place (Oxford Archaeology, 2004). This is apparently confirmed in the copious notes of no lesser person than William Smith – known as the 'Father of English Geology'. In 1811 he described the Combe Down Freestone Quarries noting: "*The process of quarrying freestone is conivened by making a passage...down to the face of the rock through the rubble and rag which lies over it.*" Having thus exposed the face, a quarrymaster had the option of surface quarrying, which required the removal of all the 'ridding' overlying the freestone, or 'mining'. As Smith records: "*If quarried underground the workmen begin holing under the Rag in the upper beds of the Freestone which are called the picking stuff – This holing about 4 feet high is called picking...*" (Smith Papers, Univ. of Oxford Museum Library). The accompanying sketch of a '*Section of Stone Northside the Down*' is almost certainly a representation of this quarry face adjacent to Bradford Road (fig.12).

Abraham Sumsion would almost certainly have been engaged, together with his neighbours Henry Street and John Scrace, in the excavation of this quarry 'trench'. Whether subsequently he chose to surface quarry or to mine, a crane (used to lift stone) and windlass (used to move stone horizontally) would be essential pieces of equipment in order to haul the stone to road level. Later, when sufficient space became available, an incline could be built to achieve this purpose. In 1809, the year Abraham Sumsion died, his neighbour, **John Scrace**, was declared bankrupt and all his land, property, goods and chattels were advertised for auction (Bath Chronicle, 14th December, 1809). Amongst these goods was "*a share or use in a crane and two windlasses*" at his quarry in Combe Down. The simple geography and logic of the situation suggests Scrace, if sharing a crane, must have been working side by side with Sumsion, and that the area of operation was the northern end of their respective strips of land. Later, once quarried out and backfilled, the land could be used for building construction. Indeed, the Rate Books and architectural evidence suggest most if not all the cottages on this site were built before 1825. They were most likely constructed to house quarry workers and thus 'faced' south, away from the road, in the direction of the continuing quarry operations.

John Scrace somehow overcame his financial difficulties and continued to operate his quarry next to Combe Road until the early 1830s. Apart from the information that can be gleaned from the notices of bankruptcy, however, there is very little else available to shed light on this rather enigmatic character. A deed in private possession does describe Scrace's initial purchase from Salmon in July, 1803, but this document describes him, intriguingly, as a '*shoemaker*' from the City of Bath. Quite why a shoemaker would wish to make the transition to quarrymaster is unclear, although just over a century later it was a grocer, Augustus Thatcher Cox, who was to lend his name to the quarries here. Perhaps this was merely a speculative venture, and Scrace employed a ganger to supervise the actual work. More likely, the quarry was operated by a son of John Scrace the Shoemaker, also named John, who was or had been apprenticed to a Combe Down stonemason. If so, a likely candidate for teacher or master is Henry Street Snr., since both are recorded in the LW Parish Rate Books as living at Crossway Place, near the top of Entry Hill. John Scrace makes his first appearance in the Rate Books in September, 1804, alongside the other quarrymasters of LW Byfield. In 1809 he is charged rates for both a house and quarry, being only the second to achieve this status after Henry Street. In fact it appears from William Smith's papers that Henry Street was rebuilding his property around this time, probably with the assistance of John Scrace, and that both took a share of the new premises – named Crossway Place. The relative grandeur of the property is evidenced by the fact that Street and Scrace were each charged 6s./9d. for rates whereas Nowell (from 1810) and Mrs. Rudman (from 1812) were only charged 2s./3d. for their more humble abodes. Scrace's property, which adjoined Street's, was described as Lot 3 in the Notice of Sale by Auction following his declared bankruptcy in December 1809:

LOT 3

All the FREEHOLD MESSUAGE or DWELLING HOUSE
with a large piece of GROUND adjoining, ...situate at a place
called CROSSWAY PLACE on Coomb Down in the said parish
of Widcombe; now and for some time past in the possession of
the said John Scrace, the bankrupt

(Bath Chronicle, 14th Dec., 1809).

The sale never actually took place, presumably because Scrace was able to clear himself from the position of bankruptcy. However, the Rate Books suggest that his ownership of a house at Crossway Place became less certain for a while. In 1817 it is noted that the house occupied by Scrace was only valued at 2s./9d. and that it was owned by Henry Street. In 1819 he apparently no longer occupied Crossway Place at all, and in 1821 and 1822 the name of John Scrace disappears from the Rate Book altogether (as did the names Hulonce and Rudman from time to time). By 1825, when the Rate Books were, for the first time, arranged according to place of residence rather than by name, John Scrace remerges as owner of two of the three properties at Crossway Place, Henry Street being owner-occupier of the other, all of them having a rate charged at 6s./9d. The precise agreements between Scrace and Street are not known, but seem to have included preparedness by both parties to loan money to the other on the security of ownership of the Crossway Place properties.

With regard to his business activity, no evidence has come to light to link John Scrace with any particular building project outside Combe Down. The fact he must have been engaged in building construction is confirmed once again, however, in the various announcements made in local newspapers at the time of his bankruptcy in 1809. In November of that year, seemingly before he had been declared a bankrupt, the following notice appeared in the Bath Journal:

TO BE SOLD BY AUCTION...
AT THE FULL MOON near the OLD BRIDGE, Bath on TUESDAY evening Nov. 14th at eight o'clock SIX Thousand STOURBRIDGE BRICKS in lots of 300 each now lying on Bath Quay. For a view of the same, apply to Mr SALMON on the Quay, or to Mr JOHN SCRACE, Coomb Down

(Bath Journal, November 1809, p3 col 2).

It seems that John Scrace had agreed to engage on a building project, somewhere in Bath, and that he had ordered a shipment of bricks accordingly. The fact they were Stourbridge Bricks is significant, for these are well-known as special quality firebricks for use in ovens or fireplaces. Was Scrace planning to build a whole terrace of houses – perhaps on the scale of Devonshire buildings? No doubt he was busy in the meantime quarrying stone for the project at Combe Down. Perhaps he was already on the construction site preparing foundations, or an even later stage of building. Whatever, having been instructed to pay cash on delivery of the bricks, and owing his quarry and construction workers their wages, it seems the building contract was cancelled and that there was no immediate prospect of any payment to himself. He had a serious cash-flow problem and action was taken to declare him a bankrupt – perhaps initiated by the supplier of the bricks. Offering the bricks for immediate sale – no doubt at a cut-down price – gave Scrace a temporary lifeline. Within a month, however, his house and other property, including his quarry, was being offered for sale in order to recoup the rest of his debts. Life was never easy for a quarrymaster! For Mr. Salmon, hired presumably to act as agent for John Scrace, life was perhaps not so hard.

The fact that John Scrace never did feature in a major, even memorable building project does not necessarily imply that his quarry was in any way unsuccessful. The major contracts which did appear from time to time might demand quantities of stone that were beyond the abilities of an individual quarrymaster to supply in a limited time frame. As a result, contracts for supply of stone were almost certainly shared between neighbouring quarrymasters. The position of John Scrace's quarry in the centre of the LW and MC Byfield complex could very possibly have worked to his advantage in this respect.

It seems clear that once Scrace had excavated his section of the quarry, or trench, at the corner of Bradford Road and Combe Road he opted to 'mine' the freestone by 'holing a picking bed'. This is suggested by both archaeological evidence (Oxford Archaeology, 2004), and by the 1839 LW Tithe Map (fig. 6). In fact there are two levels of underground workings leading off the quarry face at this point, both heading south, parallel to Combe Road. This is a rare, if not the only occurrence of multi-tiered working in the Firs-Byfield complex, and possible reasons for it are worth investigating. First, William Smith notes that the beds of freestone on this north side of the Down were very 'thick', the bottom beds being the 'hardest'. Second, there seems to be evidence to suggest that along this northern section of Combe Road there may have been instances where quarrymasters transgressed the parish boundary. This opens up the question of whether or not it was Scrace who excavated both levels, or whether he permitted neighbouring quarrymasters, working from the Monkton Combe side of the boundary, to extend their workings into Scrace's property (and vice versa?). The proposition seems at first an unlikely one, but there is evidence that between 1811 and 1815 others (i.e. not any of the original six LW Byfield quarrymasters) may have been quarrying in the Byfield area at a very small scale.

From 1811 or so there is a small rise in the number of people paying quarry rates according to the Lyncombe and Widcombe Rate Books. Most are on quarries located elsewhere, such as at Entry Hill where Mr. Bennett was the likely owner, but two names stand out for the fact that they were working quarries 'owned' by Mr. Salmon. They were Mssrs. Shephard and Bolwell, and both paid a rate of just 1s./6d., or one quarter the amount paid by the LW Byfield masters on the other 'Salmon' quarries. It is, of course, quite possible that Mr. Salmon had invested in the opening up of quarries elsewhere, but it is also reasonable to conclude that Shephard and Bolwell were paying a 'token' rate for the right to extend their existing quarries into Lyncombe and Widcombe parish (adding fuel to the suggestion that MC Byfield was more or less worked out by this time). Until such time that we learn more of the Monkton Combe quarrymasters of this period we may never be certain. What is clear is that both Shephard and Bolwell ceased paying quarry rates by 1816. Meanwhile John Scrace continued to pay the 'full' quarry rate of 6s. until he also disappeared from the books for a while in the early 1820s. An interesting aside to this story is the fact that the years of this upswing in quarrying activity coincide with the time William Smith himself ventured into the stone extraction business and opened his own, ill-fated Kingham Field Quarry on the south side of the Down, along Summer Lane (Winchester, 2001).

By 1825 the Rate Books show Scrace had built and owned some cottages along Combe Road, including, and in the immediate vicinity of Spring Cottage. Probably Scrace had surface quarried this section of his property, prior to leveling it by filling it with waste stone, and rendering it "*fit for the plough*". Such terms of contract were standard at this time for all land leased or sold for the purpose of quarrying. At least one more cottage was built in 1826 (private deeds), although Scrace continued to pay quarry rates until 1831. It appears that he died shortly after then, and by 1833 his family had completely disappeared from the Byfield area (LW Parish Rate Books). What remains unclear is precisely to what extent he quarried stone underground and how much of his land was surface quarry. Probably the Tithe Map gives a fairly accurate impression of the extent to which he 'mined' stone, being restricted to the north end of Combe Road where the access road to the old quarry workings is now. Further south he seems to have preferred to operate an open quarry, in the same way that his neighbour and probable mentor Henry Street conducted his business.

Henry Street has been mentioned in this narrative a number of times already. Henry Senior was one of the original quarrymasters on Green Down, having interests at Crossway Place as well as Byfield. He retired as a quarrymaster early in 1814, passing management of his extensive quarries over to his son, Henry Junior, before his death in or about 1820 (LW Parish Rate Books). Henry Junior then carried on digging stone uninterrupted until he sold his quarries in 1850 to his son-in-law Philip Nowell. The 'quarry', by this time covering much of the western half of the former LW Byfield quarries, continued in operation for many decades afterwards, mostly under the guise of Cox's Quarry. Henry Junior is described as a "*retired quarrymaster and proprietor of houses*" in the 1851 Population Census, still living at Crossway Place. He is distinguished by the fact that he is the only one of the original six LW Byfield quarrymasters to have a quarry named after him in Addison's list of 41 Combe Down quarries (Addison, 1998). In fairness to Street, however, it has to be said that Addison's description of the quarry and its erstwhile ownership hardly does justice to this most important and enduring of Byfield quarrymasters.

A little of what we know about Henry Street and his quarries derives from William Smith. It is no surprise that, as the 'Father of English Geology' Smith should be interested in describing details of all quarrying activity that he might come across. Also, at the time he was making notes on Combe Down, around 1811, he was probably contemplating opening up a quarry of his own nearby. Smith was clearly a guest of Street, for he describes both the Crossway Place and the Byfield quarries in some detail. He also made notes on the newly dug well at Crossway Place, observing that it *"was sunk through the bottom of the Rock at the new House at Entry Hill ... which produces the Crossway paving stone"*. This paving stone attracted a great deal of his attention, for he also wrote a four page note entitled *"Great Oolite – Paving Stone of the Crossway, on Entry Hill 1Mile South of Bath"*. As well as informing us of the nature of the Oolite here – it dipped at an angle *'near 45 Degrees to the horizon'* – he provides us a major clue as to the nature and purpose of this small quarry. Whereas other quarries might focus on the production of ashlar blocks for walls, or weather-proof stone for sills and footings, Crossway Place produced the paving slabs for stone floors. Whilst not as durable as the Pennant Sandstone or Caithness Flags laid down on the more fashionable or heavily used pedestrian and vehicular areas in Bath, the supply of domestic paving slabs was clearly a vital element of the local building industry (Devon, Parkins, and Workman, 2001; 8-9). The quarry seems still to have been active at the time of Smith's visit(s), but it is rarely mentioned in other documentary sources. Possibly, once Street had begun opening up his Byfield quarry workings, he only quarried enough paving stone to meet current orders. Whatever, the Crossway Place Quarry was clearly an extremely useful and no doubt profitable venture for Street, setting him up as perhaps the pre-eminent quarrymaster on the Down in the late 1790s.

William Smith also described Street's Byfield Quarry workings:

Mr. Streets Quarrys -
These Quarries have lately been opened at a most enormous Expense - occasioned partly by the great quantity of rubbish by which the Freestone is covered and partly by the excavation and removal to a great distance of very large course blocks of Rag which is called the Cockly Bed.
No such stone as this was ever before found in any Quarries on the Down.
This bed of stone further westward gets 6 or 7 feet thick.
Blocks of 20 Tons each may be got from these Quarries -
7.4 Cube yd. = 5ft.10in. side of the Cube = 12.5 Tons Weight.

A number of points can be inferred from these notes. It is clear, of course, that Street was surface quarrying – that is, he removed all the overlying '*rubbish*' rock and ragstone in order to extract blocks of freestone. After the quarry face was well established removal of waste rubble became less of a problem. Once the initial trench had been excavated the overburden, or 'ridding', was simply tipped into the void created as the quarry face moved forward. In order to prevent the waste rocks rolling forward on to the face and face-workers a series of roughly built walls were constructed, advancing just a few yards behind the face. It was this arrangement which necessitated the system of elevated plank walkways to wheel the barrows carrying the waste into position, as graphically described by Beazer (1981, 85). The problem at Street's quarry appears to have been that the initial volume of Cockly 'ridding' was too great for immediate disposal locally and so had to be removed to '*a great distance*', possibly by expensive horse and cart. Crossway Place may have offered a site for this debris and, presumably, Street regularly hauled building stone there anyway while he was constructing his new house.

The obvious question raised here is why did Street not save this 'enormous expense' by quarrying under the Cockly Bed? If indeed it was so hard, and lay to a depth of up to 7 feet, it should have provided a firm enough ceiling to allow underground quarrying. After all, John Scrace, Street's immediate neighbour to the east, was able to mine at two vertically separate levels! The important point to bear in mind, however, is that the state of the rocks could vary considerably over even a relatively small area of the Down. The conditions noted by Smith had never before been found "*in any quarries on the Down*". Beazer is also at pains to point out that "*Stone from the Combe Down quarries varied … one could not really generalize as there were pockets of good stone to be found over the whole area just as there were pockets of defective stone*" (Beazer, 1981, 86). Perhaps Street simply did not feel confident enough to undermine this variable Cockly Bed, no doubt hoping that for most of his intended quarry the cost of removal of overburden would not be so high. Also, it is clear that the quality of freestone he uncovered was remarkably good, at least when measured in terms of the size of blocks he was able to excavate. Indeed it may be the case that he felt such blocks could only be dug out by first removing the overlying rocks, and that extraction via underground roadways would be impractical.

One possibility is that Street initially did attempt underground quarrying, and then gave up in favour of surface quarrying. It has already been postulated that Street's first quarry venture in the Byfield area was to the west of Greendown Place, in the area where the Foresters Pub now stands. The Tithe Map (fig. 6) suggests the north-west corner of this plot had been surface quarried, and also that the adjacent plots to the immediate south and east had been undermined (Plots 512 and 514). The relative size of these plots suggests that underground headings were only pushed out a few yards in each direction from the open quarry, as one might expect with exploratory workings. A little further south, at Plot 511, the ground was once again opened up to surface excavation. It was here, according to Smith, that the thickness of the Cockly Bed was greatest, yet it is clear that Street decided this was not an appropriate location to pursue underground quarrying. Instead, it appears that he preferred to concentrate his quarrying further east, initially (after 1803) on land he purchased from Salmon, then (after 1809) on the land formally belonging to the late Abraham Sumsion.

The question of whether or not Street did open up the Widcombe Field Quarry just west of Greendown Place in the late 18th century is still not resolved with absolute certainty, however. Of interest is the fact that Smith's description refers to Street's '*quarrys*' rather than a singular quarry. That the plural was indeed intended is confirmed in a deed of sale dated 1812 in which Street sold a small plot of land adjacent to the Bradford Road for use as a Jewish Burial Ground (Bath City Archives, Box11/291). This land had almost certainly served as Street's first quarry 'trench' after the 1803 purchase, and had subsequently been backfilled and covered with a layer of topsoil. A small margin map on the deed confirms that the plot is at the northern end of Street's quarry, purchased from Salmon in 1803 (fig. 13). Typically for such plans, it also shows the land immediately adjacent to Street's plot. To the east (mistakenly drawn as west on the plan!) is also land belonging to Mr. Street. This was the property purchased after Abraham Sumsions death in 1809. On the other three sides are roads: Bradford Road to the north; Mr. Salmon's 'intended' 12ft. road to the south; and "*a road 15 and a half feet wide Leading to Mr. Street's Quarries*" to the west. This latter road is modern Greendown Place. The text of the deed is more specific, describing the road as leading to the "*two Stone Quarries now worked by the said Henry Street*". What is unclear is whether one of these quarries is on the land which was formerly Sumsion's. If so, it has to be said that the road in question does not lead directly to this land. It does lead, however, to land on the other, western side of the road where, it is proposed, Street's earlier Widcombe Field Quarry would have been. Unfortunately, in keeping with the contemporary style of these maps, ownership of this land is not recorded since it is not immediately adjacent to the land being transferred, and so is not relevant to the deed of transferal.

In 1814 the Parish Rate Books declare Henry Street Senior to be the owner-occupier of the house at Crossway Place, and Henry Street Junior to be owner-occupier of the quarry. Clearly the elder Street had retired. Henry Junior was at this time aged in his mid to late 30s, and apparently unmarried. He had his own quarry underground in MC Byfield, and in 1813 had secured the right of wayleave from William Hulonce to use the underground passageways leading from Ralph Allen's Yard to LW Byfield. It seems most likely that he was shifting his area of working at this time from MC Byfield (possibly by now worked out) to the underground area formerly sold by Hulonce to Abraham Sumsion and now owned by his father. It is possible that this area had never been worked at all since, as William Smith indicates, Henry Senior had been kept so busy with his surface quarries adjoining Bradford Road and Greendown Place. The wayleave secured by Henry Junior in 1813 could only have been used to facilitate his quarrying this underground resource. The retirement of his father then allowed Henry Junior the freedom to open up the so-called 'Byfield Mine Entrance' further west, allowing him to extract the stone blocks in either direction. Henry Senior died about 1820 and, in quick succession, Henry Junior took possession of Crossway Place, married, and sired at least four children (three daughters and a son). He continued working all the Street quarries, uninterrupted, until his own retirement in 1850, aged over 70.

Hard Times

Following the Allied victory over Napoleon's forces at Waterloo in June, 1815, the Duke of Wellington's army stepped ashore in England to a hero's welcome. It is quite possible that some soldiers and sailors returned to their family homes in Combe Down, perhaps even hoping to find work in the quarries. Had they done so, they would soon have realized that the celebrations had a hollow ring, for the nation was actually sinking into a state of real and protracted depression. School-day memories resound with phrases dictated by history masters as they droned about the years after Waterloo: "Peterloo"; "Corn Laws"; and the "Combination Acts". "The Madness of King George". "1816 was 'the year without a summer'". "Luddism"; "Industrial Mechanisation"; "The Factory System"; and "Commons' Enclosure" all had relevance in this period still. It was a period which Sellar and Yeatman (1930) may well have described as "A Bad Thing".

Locally, there was depression in the agricultural sector as well as in the historically important wool and lace industries. In fact the latter two activities virtually disappeared in Somerset and the South-West at this time (Berg, 1994). The important thing to realize is that this period of economic collapse affected not just the labouring classes, but masters as well; and some speculators, and land-owners, and a few landed gentry too – though not all suffered equally. In this period of no-confidence amidst economic uncertainty the desire to invest in new projects, and expensive building projects especially, crumbled. The cancellation of intended projects, as well as the cessation of works at on-going projects, had an immediate and often devastating impact on the builders themselves. In Bath and environs this meant the quarrymasters and all those engaged in the quarry trade. Famously, the 'father of English geology' – William Smith – was forced into debtors' prison during the post-Waterloo years due to the failure of his 'Combe Down quarry' at Kingham Field (Winchester, 2001; 245-252). The question is to what extent were the hardships that befell William Smith reflected in the circumstances of the Byfield quarrymasters?

The threat of bankruptcy was familiar to John Scrace, at least. In 1809 he suffered a severe cash-flow crisis and was declared bankrupt by court order and all his land, goods, and chattels offered for sale in the local press. He seems to have survived, however, having suffered no more than dented pride, and there is no evidence that he was ever imprisoned. His experience was most likely put down to 'one of those things' that can happen anytime in business. Apparently, he was able to sort out his affairs and get back to work in his quarry in a remarkably short space of time. During 1821 and 1822, however, he appears to have ceased quarrying altogether (LW Parish Rate Books). Was *this* an indication of difficulties facing the industry at this time? Sophia Rudman also disappears from the Rate Books, but for an extended period from 1820 to 1824. In her case the newspapers do record a notice of bankruptcy issued against her, in October, 1819. She is described as '*late* of the Parish of Lyncombe and Widcombe', implying that she had moved from the area – possibly to debtors prison? (Bath Chronicle, 7th October, 1819). Of note in both these cases is the relative lateness in this period of economic slow-down before they succumbed to bankruptcy and/or the cessation of production.

This is not the case with William Hulonce who, having already disposed of more than half his original land holding, apparently ceased production in 1816 and did not resume again until 1822 (LW Parish Rate Books). Of particular interest in this case is a mortgage taken out by Hulonce in 1818, for £200, taken against the security of his remaining quarry land at LW Byfield. The money lender was Mr. James Gooden, a '*school-master of Bath*', and the interest rate was fixed at 5% per annum. Annual interest payments were apparently made on time each year (on November 30th), so that in 1821 Mr. Gooden felt sufficiently comfortable to extend the loan by a further £100. After then interest and capital repayments seem to have ceased for considerable periods, since by 1851 the total debt amounted to more than £413 (Bath City Archives, MH/7/16). Hulonce's land was eventually forfeited, suggesting that the family had borrowed to stave off disaster rather than invest in any kind of new project. Even though Hulonce did return to quarrying in 1822 it does seem the family had indeed suffered the adverse effects of the economic slump following Waterloo. Although possibly unrelated, a rather cryptic comment in the Rate Book for August, 1831 notes that William Hulonce (probably Junior) was '*in prison*' (and thus unable to pay rates!). Details are lacking, unfortunately, but there is one more case of prison incarceration where the unfortunate situation of one more Byfield quarrymaster is documented at some length.

Patrick Byrne had become a Byfield quarrymaster when he acquired part of Hulonce's land just two days after the original purchase from Salmon in August 1805. His land occupied one acre at the westernmost end of Hulonce's original plot (fig. 7). (It is easily recognized today as the former quarry ground *facing* the 'Byfield Mine Entrance', where access for the enabling works for the Stabilization Project exists at this time of writing.) Byrne was an established quarryman, associated most closely with construction work for the Kennet and Avon Canal. The General Committee Minute Book for 1802 records payments to Patrick Byrne for stone supplied for building locks at Bath on a number of occasions, the stone having been extracted from the Kennet and Avon 'Company' quarry on Claverton Down (Public Record Office, RAIL 842/2). Later, in 1811, he provided stone for the New Bridewell at Devizes. A total of four shipments of stone enabled Patrick Byrne to receive a total payment of £477 (Wiltshire CRO A4/2/5/6/4). His association with more than one quarry may explain why Byrne does not appear in the Lyncombe and Widcombe Rate Books until 1808, when he is charged the same rate as the other Byfield quarrymasters for his quarrying activities (1s.6d. at that time). He is also recorded as resident in the Parish, although the precise location of his home is not clear. In 1812, at a time when the fortunes of the quarrying industry seemed good generally, he is shown to have paid rates for a '*warf*', in addition to payment for his 'Byfield' quarry, and '*land*'. He seems indeed to have been a quarrymaster with ambition! For every £4 he paid in quarry rates, a further £3 were paid for his wharf facilities – located, no doubt, close by the locks for which he had provided stone, and possibly constructed with his own hands.

After 1815 a familiar pattern begins to emerge. In the Rate Books for November 1816 Patrick Byrne is described as '*late*'. Subsequent entries have no mention of a quarry (in the same way that other quarrymasters such as Scrace and Rudman also disappeared from the records for a while), although he continued to bear the "late" appellation for the '*warf*' entry until the early 1820s. Other records (embodied in deed portfolios maintained privately) indicate that in May, 1815, Byrne secured a mortgage of £160 from Mr. E. Salmon - £60 to be repaid within six months, with interest, and the remaining £100 within the following year, with interest. The question arises once again, just as with Hulonce, was the loan intended to tide over a period of temporary difficulty, or was it to help finance a new project? In terms of the remuneration gained from the Bridewell project at Devizes the sum borrowed from Salmon seems quite small. Perhaps this, in a way, helps quantify the difference in economic circumstance between the pre- and post-Waterloo eras. Byrnes failure to repay his debt to Salmon led him back, ironically, to a rather different 'bridewell'. In late 1817 Salmon called his dues, and Byrne, just a few months before William Smith, was incarcerated in the Fleet Prison in London as a bankrupt debtor. In the eyes of society at that time failure to pay back borrowed or owed money meant that he was regarded as little better than a common thief.

Byrne's 'crime', and his subsequent release from gaol, is recorded in a later (1825) deed of transfer of property:

> ... *And reciting that the said Patrick Byrne being indebted to sundry persons in more money than he was able to pay he had been arrested and confined as a debtor in the Fleet Prison from whence he was discharged in the month of June 1818 under and by virtue of the powers and provisions contd in a Statute made and passed in the 53rd year of the reign of his then late Majesty King George the 3rd entitled "An Act for the Relief of Insolvent Debtors in England"* ...

In other words, 'mad' King George had recognized the insanity of incarcerating insolvent debtors when imprisonment meant no solution could be found for prisoners to sort out their debts while thus incarcerated. But how was the debt to be resolved once the debtor had received the King's pardon? In the case of this ex-con a new indenture was made on "*the twelfth day of August in the year of our Lord 1818* **Between Edward Salmon** *of the City of Bath Gentleman of the one part and* **Patrick Byrne** *of the Parish of Bathford ... quarry man of the other part ...*". First, Edward Salmon stated his case: that "*no part of the said principal sum of one hundred and sixty pounds nor any interest thereon*" had been paid by Byrne, so that the total now owing was "*the sum of one hundred and eighty five pounds and twelve shillings for principal and interest monies ...*". The solution was that *Byrne's* quarry, now in the possession of Salmon (since the land had been offered as security for the loan), should be leased to Byrne – but under certain, very strict conditions. These terms seem truly remarkable to our modern eyes!

The lease was to be for seven years, with an annual rent payment of £19 to be paid in twice-yearly installments. Byrne was to assume full responsibility for payment of land taxes and so on, "*...and perform all parish and personal duties in respect of the said plot of ground ...*". The terms then stipulated that, if Byrne was to quarry the land, he should:

> '... *quarry or dig out the said land regularly, commencing from the eastward end ... as specified in the plan hereon* (a margin map shows the land divided into five roughly equal strips, denoting the sequence in which the land should be quarried) ...*and in no other way and ... before the expiration of the term hereby granted level the whole surface of the ground either by filling up*

such quarry or otherwise throwing arches over the same and shall carry away or otherwise bury all the loose stone and rubbish ... and effectually level the surface thereof so as to level throughout such part as shall have been quarried not more than five feet below nor more than five feet above the present level of the ground unquarried next adjoining the westward boundary wall and shall reserve and set apart from the rubbish all midden mould (topsoil) which he shall dig from the surface of the ground for the purpose of quarrying under the same, and after the land shall have been quarried out and levelled shall spread the same mould or other good mould to be brought for that purpose from other places regularly not less than three quarters of a foot thick over the whole surface of the rubbish and levelled ground so as to render the whole of the said plot of ground fit for agriculture or garden ground.

The terms regarding restoration of the land after quarrying are not at all unusual, although only rarely have local deeds survived which express these conditions with such clarity. They highlight, if nothing else, the enormous logistic problems which might be encountered by those who opted to surface quarry rather than quarry underground. The instruction regarding the sequence of quarrying is unusual, however. It would seem to indicate that perhaps the quality of stone here was not uniformly good, or that some parts of the plot were more difficult to quarry than others. Even today it seems the plot has never been fully quarried out. Was this a form of 'punishment' for Byrne, or merely a means of ensuring that all good quality stone would or could eventually be extracted? The terms imposed on Byrne continue:

And also (he) *shall and will within one year from the day of the date hereof dig or otherwise sink a well of sufficient depth to supply a good supply of water for a dwelling house and well and effectually wall the sides of the same from top to bottom **And also** shall and will within three years ... erect ... or cause to be erected and built and finished one good ashlar or rough stone and timber messuage or dwelling house to be well faced and to be of not less value than one hundred and fifty pounds when finished **And also** shall and will quit and deliver up the said plot of ground and all improvements erections and buildings to be made or built therein or thereon unto the said Edward Salmon ... at the expiration of the term hereby granted.*

Such was the cost of a King's Pardon! It must be noted, however, that the conditions further stipulated that if indeed the house was completed, and if the work was to the satisfaction of the City of Bath Architect (John Fusden), future rental payments would be reduced by half for the remainder of the seven year term. If any of the conditions were to be broken, on the other hand, Patrick Byrne would straightway be declared Bankrupt again in the London Gazette. Even by the standards of the day, Edward Salmon must have been judged a hard man though, given the stigma attached to unattended debt, just.

Patrick Byrne was able to make some repayment of his initial loan but, almost at the end of his seven year term, Edward Salmon declared he was still owed, with all interest paid, the sum of £150. 9s. 9d. Fortunately for Byrne, Salmon found a purchaser for the land who was willing to pay £154. 9s. 9d. Salmon, it seems, had obtained his pound of flesh and Byrne was released from further ignominy. There is no record of either house or well ever being constructed. The new owner was Robert Langman, a quarryman from Monkton Combe Parish, but in 1824 he too realised that this piece of land, still largely unquarried, was unlikely ever to produce rich profits. He sold the land for exactly the same price he had purchased at two years earlier to, of all people, a dentist, Isaac Willson, from Bath. The investment proved a wise one, surprisingly, for one year later, in September 1825, the quarry was re-sold to a certain James Byfield, haullier, for the sum of £185.

From about 1824 the fortunes of the Byfield quarrymasters seem generally to have taken a turn for the better. By this time Scrace, Rudman and Hulonce had all resumed quarrying, and the feeling of buoyancy in the community was reflected, and no doubt lifted, by the building of a hostelry near the old 'Ralph Allen's Yard' in the same year. This was the public house soon after to be known as the King William IV (LW Parish Rate Books). James Byfield, who earned his living hauling the stone from the quarries to the canal-side wharves would certainly have welcomed this upturn in fortune. In fact it all seems to have rather gone to his head, for he determined that his own path to fortune lay in quarrying as well as carting. So it was that he bought Patrick Byrne's old quarry.

Unfortunately, virtually no evidence remains to tell us the story of the 'true' Byfield quarry. Surviving deeds, in private possession, suggest that for the first few years all seems to have gone well – or maybe not! It was not until early in 1830 that James Byfield was forced to take out a mortgage, like so many before him, for the not inconsiderable sum of £450. Repayment, with interest, was expected within one year. In 1841, "*several mortgage securities later*", Byfield owed a grand total of £1647 14s. This quarry, which was really not worth anything near this sum, was a proven route to disaster, and was almost certainly the literal death of James Byfield. The quarry was repossessed in 1841, probably just after Byfield's demise and, subsequently, the Bath and Cheltenham Gazette, 19th April, 1842, offered the following notice of sale:

VALUABLE QUARRY GROUND
... To be Sold by Auction ... On APRIL 21
LOT I. All that PLOT of GROUND situate on COOMB DOWN, containing One Acre, late in the occupation of Mr. James Byfield. About 14 perch of the above Ground has not been Quarried, and contains Beds of Freestone, of the first quality. - The above premises are held for a Term of which 363 Years are unexpired.

This advertisement fooled no-one, and no-one wished to buy. The money-lender/vendor, Mr. J. Graves, a 'gentleman' of Bath, had to wait a further six years before he could finally rid himself of this land. In 1848 it was sold to Richard Lankesheer, *'quarrymaster of Bath'*. This Lankesheer was most probably the son, or possibly grandson of the Richard Lankesheer who had worked MC Byfield from the entrance at Ralph Allen's Yard in the 1790s and early 1800s. It was probably the same Richard Lankesheer who, according to the 1851 Monkton Combe Tithe Map, had opened a quarry to the north of Bradford Road, near the Hadley Arms pub, shortly before this time. The amount he paid J. Graves was a paltry £49. Just a month or two later he sold the quarry to Henry Street, who owned most of the adjoining land, for the unaccountably knock-down price of £45.

Good Times

In the early 1800s the task of building a humble stone dwelling-house was, in most cases, left entirely in the hands of the builder, who was invariably the stone-mason, and who was possibly also the quarrymaster who excavated the stone. Rough designs may have been drawn up, but builders relied more on instinct and experience than carefully drawn architectural plans. In the case of Patrick Byrne, for example, he was obliged to construct a house first, *then* have it certified as properly built by the City Architect. Grander residences, such as Devonshire Buildings, would require the services of an architect, and such services were most definitely required for large-scale public works projects as well as for the stately homes of the noble classes. Architects of the day gained their reputations from the patronage of members of the nobility, and through recommendation to other members of Parliament and thus to the controllers of the public purse. The highest accolades of all (and the most visible and lucrative building projects) were reserved for that elite group of architects who enjoyed Royal patronage. In the age of the Regency (1811-1830) this meant attracting the eye and the favour of the Prince of Wales, erstwhile Regent and, from 1820, regaled as King George IV.

The architects of many fine buildings of this era are invariably recorded in history as having 'built' the products of their imagination. Sir Christopher Wren, for example, 'built' St. Pauls Cathedral in London. This of course is nonsense, for the architect only *conceived* the grand plan. However praiseworthy the effort involved in producing sketched concepts, and however formidable the production of detailed architectural drawings may have been, few architects ever dirtied their hands (once their reputations had been established) chiseling stone or applying bricks to mortar. On any major building project the architect would produce detailed plans and then appoint a Clerk of Works to ensure the actual building work was carried out to specification. In fact the Clerk of Works was really more of an administrator than a builder: cajoling bankers, disbursing payments, mentally calculating flow-charts, and hiring and firing labourers. The architect would specify by name the specialist artists and craftsmen he wished to engage on a project. He would also elect the chief builders who would engage in, as well as supervise, the actual building work. Chief among these men was invariably *the* stone mason, or master mason. The stone mason was also responsible for the placing of orders for stone and, unless the architect issued specific instructions to the contrary, held a reasonably free rein when determining which quarry should provide the stone. This fact is the key to understanding the overall fortunes of the Byfield Mine, and the role these quarries played in shaping England's architectural heritage during the Regency.

In 1806 an up-and-coming architect named Jeffrey Wyatt, aged 40 years, was commissioned to begin major extension work at Longleat, the home of Thomas Thynne, the Second Marquess of Bath. Wyatt held an advantage over most contemporaries in his profession in that he was the nephew of, and had been apprenticed to, one of the most famous architects in the land at that time – James Wyatt. James had studied in Venice and acquired a fondness for the Palladian style, which Ralph Allen also followed when planning his Prior Park Estate. James went on to establish his reputation with renovation work to cathedrals throughout England, including Salisbury, Lichfield, and Durham. From 1786 to 1789 James Wyatt was architect for Beckford's ill-fated scheme at Fonthill Abbey. Following collapse of the first structure in 1791 the 'Abbey' was reconstructed using Bath stone (instead of concrete) to face the building. Jeffrey, then in his mid-twenties, was recruited to assist his uncle at this stage and it is during this period that he would almost certainly have met some Combe Down quarrymasters and stone masons. Although Jeffrey had been born in the Midlands (Burton-on-Trent), and was later associated with many fine buildings in that part of the country (notably he designed the north wing extension to Chatsworth House), he became best known, and was eventually knighted for, buildings he worked upon in southern England using Bath stone. Having become independent in 1799 he worked on the renovation to the Manor House at Nonsuch Park in Surrey between 1801 and 1806 as well as other projects involving fashionable country houses. It was undoubtedly one of these projects which attracted the attention of the Marquess of Bath.

The Longleat project was a major one. Initially it involved construction of a new north wing in a style compatible with the rest of the house. It was later extended, possibly as a result of Wyatt's highly persuasive influence on the Marquess, to include extensive remodeling of the original house interior and the building and associated landscaping of a new stable block and orangery (Burnett, 1978). The whole project was eventually to last 12 years, finishing in 1818. As architect, of course, Wyatt was free to move around the country at this time and engage on other projects: Phillips House in Wiltshire; Browsholme Hall in Lancashire; Kelmarsh Rectory in Northamptonshire; and Ashridge at Berkhampstead - to name just a few. To ensure the works at Longleat were carried out according to his plans, Wyatt simply had to appoint a competent Clerk of Works and a trustworthy builder, or master mason. The mason he appointed was Philip Nowell, third son of Samuel Nowell, aged just 25 years.

Work at Longleat began in April, 1806 with the digging of foundations, the erection of timber scaffolding, and the building of brick kilns. Philip Nowell first appears in the Account Books in August of that year, when he received a fortnightly 'advance' of £5. By May 1807 he was receiving monthly payments of at least £50, suggesting he was being reimbursed for regular deliveries of stone as well as payment '*for stonemasons work (Day work only)*' (Archives, Marquess of Bath). Such monthly or bi-monthly payments continued for the next few months, until September, 1808, when much larger sums are involved suggesting the arrival of bulk shipments of stone. In that month, for example, he received £500 '*on account of the balance due to him as stonemason on bill delivered to April last*'. In December he received another £500 as payment for '*stonemason work and materials on bill to May last*'. The largest single payment was made in January, 1811, for '*stone mason and for Bath Stone etc.*' totaling £1403. 18s. 11d. Philip Nowell continued working on the Longleat project until its conclusion in 1818. He also engaged in other work for the Marquess, most notably the rebuilding of Warminster town centre in or around 1815. For this he was rewarded with the lease of four adjoining residential properties on George Street, part of a handsome terrace which he almost certainly supervised the construction of. (This terrace still stands, although the appearance has much altered since the entire stone frontage has been clad in brick!). The indenture of lease, dated 1815, was between Thomas Thynne and:

'*...Philip Nowell of Warminster ... Stone Mason of the other part witnesseth that the said Marquis for and in consideration of a surrender made by the Committee chosen for the management and superintendure [of] Monies given and subscribed for the improvement of the town of Warminster of all the ... Garden ground in part of which the Tenements or Dwelling Houses hereinafter demised are erected ...*'

The houses were described as "*No's. 4,5,6,7 of the new row of houses being on the north side of the highway lately called Chain Street now called George Street*". Annual rent was fixed at £2 for a term of 99 years or, if less, for as long as Philip or any of his three sons (Samuel, aged 11 years; Philip '*now aged about 2 yrs. and a half*'; and Arthur aged one year) should live. (The lease actually expired on the death of Philip Nowell the younger, on 2nd April, 1871.) Philip also enjoyed the lease of a builder's yard situated at the other end of the town, on East Street, near the present day, and appropriately named, Masons Arms pub. All this reflects Philip's increasing status and wealth. Even after the completion of the Longleat project he was retained by the Marquess as stonemason/builder for the Longleat Estate. Typical of the type of project he was asked to supervise were minor modifications to the Horningsham Inn, later known as the Bath Arms, in February 1821. Another, later that same year, was the repair of "*dilapidations in four houses in the market place known as Cockrell's tenement*" in Hatchet, Warminster (Archives, Marquess of Bath). Such projects were considerably smaller in scale than his previous contract, and would have had the impact of reducing the quantity of Bath Stone Philip required for his work. This, in turn, would have a negative impact on the quarries providing all this stone, especially those situated at Byfield.

As 'builder' of the extensions to Longleat House it was the responsibility of Philip Nowell to secure the supply of appropriate quantities of Bath Stone. This was of course quarried at Combe Down, where Philip's father, Samuel, was a quarrymaster at the LW Byfield site. The volume of stone required at any given time would have meant, most likely, that the work was shared around a number of quarries – although preference would always be given to Nowell's family quarry. A contract as huge as this, coupled with additional stone demanded for the Warminster urban renewal project, would have kept a number of quarrymasters in business, even through the hardships of the post 1815 economic slump. It would seem that this was the reason Rudman's and Scrace's quarries were able to keep going until 1819 at least, just after the year of completion of the Longleat project. Street's and Nowell's quarries were able to continue without cessation, the latter always assured of some business while Philip remained in the employ of the Marquess of Bath.

The 1819 Trades Directory for Bath lists the quarrymasters active in Combe Down in that year. Mr. Street of Crossway Place is mentioned, but intriguingly there is no record of his trade. Mr. R. Lankesheer is described as a stone mason, but his address is given as Claverton Street, Widcombe. Only W. Hulance (sic) is described as a quarryman, and his address is Cottage Row, Bathwick. His son *is* referred to as a stone mason of Combe Down – even though he does not appear in the Parish Rate Books at this time. There is no mention at all of Sophia Rudman, John Scrace, or Patrick Byrne. An A. Sumsion is recorded, as a mason, but he is almost certainly the only surviving quarrymaster in the non-Byfield sector of Combe Down. H. Salmon is an '*esquire*' living at Bathampton. The entry for the Nowell family is quite remarkable. Samuel Senior had died in 1816, but his sons – Samuel Junior, Jacob, and Joseph and William – are mentioned in three discrete entries (implying residence at three separate households). Samuel and Jacob are described by the somewhat unusual term '*stone-cutter*', whilst Joseph and William are '*masons*'. Although occupying separate households, it is abundantly clear that they all lived on or adjacent to their quarry site. In jubilant mood they proclaimed the name of their quarry to be '*Rockabella*'. The name shouts out the message that "Our quarry *is* working". It also 'cocks a snook' at the (presumably) more refined residents of nearby Isabella Place, who had nothing to do with quarrying at all. The Nowells were a happy crowd indeed.

Late in 1823 the Parish Rate Books suggest that changes were beginning to take place in Rockabella quarry. There is indication that Philip himself was taking charge of the site, displacing his elder brother though Samuel remained as owner of the family cottage he had inherited from their father. Perhaps Philip had been dissatisfied with aspects of the way the quarry was being run. As principal user of the stone he would certainly be concerned to ensure good quality and efficient delivery schedules. It may even be that because work had slowed down during the protracted economic depression Philip, with his new found wealth, was simply keeping the quarry 'ticking over' until major new contracts could be found. Most likely, however, Philip had become aware that a huge new contract was in the offing – one with Royal patronage – and he wanted to make sure the quarry was ready to supply at immediate request.

In 1824 Philip's old friend, the architect Jeffrey Wyatt, was commissioned by King George IV to remodel parts of Windsor Castle in addition to designing new buildings to be erected there. Essentially he was to raise the height of the Round Tower, and to build St. George's Hall, as well as a new Gatehouse. Philip Nowell was asked by Wyatt once again to be a master mason on the project. Unlike Longleat, where Philip had sole status as master mason, it seems that at Windsor at least one other work unit was formed for certain designated sections of the overall works programme. Not all the work involved Bath Stone, for example, Kentish Rag (or '*Heath*' stone) being used for much of the construction. Account Books survive for the year 1825 and these suggest that most masonry work was, in fact entrusted to Nowell, who was referred to as the '*Bath Mason*' (The National Archive, ex-PRO, Works 5/125). The same Accounts reveal that for the Midsummer Quarter of 1825 Nowell employed about ten masons, and an equal number of sawyers, labourers and so on. Unworked blocks of Bath stone to the value of £1471 lay in store, and the work which had been completed that quarter alone was worth an additional £1710, including wages. Also included was an additional bill for £16...

...Paid for a Block of Chrystal with inscription for the first stone of New Gateway laid by His Majesty on 12th August 1824 and omitted to be charged in the Xmas Quarter's Account.

The Windsor Castle project was to last four years and the impact on the neighbourhood around the Nowell quarry was inevitably wide-reaching. First, Nowell changed the name of his quarry. He clearly thought that "Rockabella" lacked sufficient grace for the Royal account books and so changed it to "Rock Hall" Quarry. Second, work was restarted in nearby quarries in the Byfield complex which had fallen to inactivity during the previous few years, since they would certainly enjoy a share of the orders Nowell was generating. 1824 was the year, of course, when even James Byfield himself was tempted to turn his hand to quarrying. Hindsight suggests he would have been far better off devoting his full attention to transportation of this stone. It would all have to be carried to Dundas wharf for trans-shipment to barge, by which it would be carried directly to Windsor via the Kennet and Avon Canal and the River Thames.

Perhaps the most lasting impact, however, was the building of a 'house and brewery' by Job (or Joab) Salter in 1824. This would be renamed the King William IV in a few years and, according to the Parish Rate Books, was easily the grandest building in this part of the Down at the time. Undoubtedly the building had the support of the local quarrymasters, including Philip Nowell, because it would be viewed as an attraction to get the best quarrymen to work here (fig. 14). Architectural evidence suggests the building frontage was extended within a few years of the original construction, and it would have been at this time that a stairway was built in the cellar leading directly to the stone mine below. It is also possible that Salter offered accommodation to some quarrymen.

The London Connection

Back in Windsor, Philip Nowell would have been aware of two other highly significant developments. In 1825 the architect John Nash submitted plans to the King for the building of the New Buckingham Palace, and work on the project proceeded later the same year (Workman, 2003). The plans called for the structure to be faced entirely in Bath Stone, and this news would certainly have been greeted most warmly in the quarries of Combe Down. It was characteristic of Nash, however, that he purchased all the stone himself and then sold it to his contractors. The choice of quarry to supply Bath stone was his, therefore, and we cannot be certain that Byfield Mine benefited in any way. What is known, from the "Report of the Commissioners appointed to visit the quarries and to enquire into the qualities of the stone to be used in the building of the New Houses of Parliament", 1839, (of which William Smith had been co-author), is that Drewes quarry at Monkton Farleigh *was* one of the providers of stone for the new Palace. Most of the Byfield quarries had closed by the time this Report was compiled, in fact, (Street's quarry was the exception) and it is perfectly possible that they also provided stone if their obligations to the Windsor Castle project allowed them. In fact completion of Nash's outer shell at Buckingham Palace, in 1828, coincided with the end of the works at Windsor Castle.

The second important development was that, coincident with the New Buckingham Palace works, and possibly because of them, the Grosvenor Estate decided to improve the area around Belgravia and Pimlico, including the expansion of wharf facilities at the Grosvenor Canal. This small waterway, reaching from the River Thames towards the heart of London, had been originally constructed in 1725 by the Chelsea Waterworks Company to provide drinking water to the then rapidly growing urban populations of Westminster, Chelsea and Kensington. Horwood's detailed survey of London in 1799 shows that, at that time, a timber yard had also been established at the northern end of the canal to facilitate supply of materials for construction of the expanding metropolis (Barker and Jackson, 1990; 88). It was the expansion of this materials supply facility, by enlargement of the canal 'basin', that was at the heart of the canal improvement scheme. It was precisely here that Nowell recognized the opportunity to bring Bath stone to London directly, via the Kennet and Avon Canal. He bought the lease on one of the new wharfs made available, and thus ensured he would get his cut on Bath Stone supplied to London before even Nash could blink an eye. Nowell's new yard, at Lower Belgrave Place, was barely a stones throw away from the New Buckingham Palace. Perhaps by this means Nowell ensured that it was he, not Nash, who remained the actual procurator of Bath stone for all Royal building works in the capital. If this is so, Rock Hall quarry would inevitably be the primary beneficiary since by now Philip himself owned the quarry (LW Parish Rate Books). The quarry must have been working at full capacity during 1824-1826, and Philip Nowell was on his way to becoming a very wealthy man.

Nowell's wharf and 'builder's yard' at Pimlico had become the long-sought entry point to the construction industry in London for Bath stone: one that Ralph Allen must have spent many years merely dreaming of. Importantly, by this route *'plain rubbed'* Bath stone could be secured in the capital for only seven-tenths the cost of its main rival – Portland stone (Report of the Commissioners for … the building of the New House of Commons, 1839). This all happened while Nowell was still engaged primarily at Windsor Castle, but it seems unlikely this prevented him from some level of involvement in construction at the new Palace. Nowell's personal contribution at Windsor included carving many Gothic details and so, as a renowned craftsman of Bath stone, and with the King himself as his patron, it seems more than likely he would have been requested to contribute his skills to the works at Buckingham Palace. According to the Official Illustrated History of the Palace:

> The exterior of Nash's Palace was faced in Bath stone. It was exquisitely detailed in a French neo-classical manner, making much use of sculptured panels and trophies, oeils-de-boeuf and carved festoons; while the principal feature of the garden front was a domed semi-circular bow… Nash's design can still be seen in the garden front of the Palace, but the entrance front, facing the Mall, is now screened from view by the new east range added by Queen Victoria in 1849.
> (Robinson, 2000; 65).

The friezes were actually accomplished in the newly developed Coade stone (Pevsner, 1957; 505) and, in any case, one wonders what exactly the relationship between Nash and Nowell may have been. Whatever, it was Nash who was eventually dismissed from the Buckingham Palace project, having infuriated the Government with massive cost overruns and his dubious business practices. An interesting aside to this affair emerges from the Public Works Account Books for 1825. Nowell assessed the cost of Bath stone delivered to Windsor at 2s.6d. per cubic foot. Nash's appointed masons on the Buckingham Palace project, Lancelot E. Wood and Manderson & Moore, assessed the Bath stone they were using at 3s.11d. per cubic foot (and Portland stone at 4s.6d.) (TNA, Works 5/125). Since, according to the Commissioners seeking stone for the new Houses of Parliament, the cost of Bath stone at the quarry site was only 6d. per cu. ft. in 1838, it is clear that transportation costs contributed most to the price of stone at the project worksite. Despite the fact that Buckingham Palace is a further one day's travel beyond Windsor Castle, this could hardly, by itself, justify Nash's claim to need to spend 35% more per block of stone than Nowell. The argument against Nash's pricing is further reinforced in an article in The Building News, dated 26th June, 1874 (p.688):

The Farleigh Down stone from the quarries of Monkton Farleigh, near Bath, ... is not suited for outside work in London.... [An] experiment on a large scale was made with Farleigh Down stone in the erection of Buckingham Palace, 50 years ago; but the decay commenced immediately after it was built; which necessitated extensive repairs and the painting of the whole of the surface with oil colour....

In the meantime, Nowell was rewarded with a new contract, in 1828, to reface the exterior of Apsley House – home to the Duke of Wellington, hero of Waterloo and Prime Minister of Great Britain, no less. It is obvious that Nowell was very much within Government favour. This time the architects were Benjamin and Philip Wyatt, and the work was to include construction of the new Corinthian portico and pediment (Pevsner, 1957; 504). Nowell would have the right to secure the stone and, once again, the quarrymen of Byfield would be celebrating. For once, though, Nowell would not be turning to his own quarry as first source of supply. In 1828 Rock Hall Quarry ceased paying quarry rates – the quarry was exhausted (LW Parish Rate Books).

Work on Apsley House finished in 1829, and it seems likely that Nowell returned to Combe Down for a while to sort out the family business and, presumably, to secure a new supply of stone. He also seems to have engaged on construction of his own home, Rock Hall, at this time. In 1831 Nowell was appointed master mason by architect Benjamin Wyatt to build the Duke of York Column at Waterloo Place, located just off The Mall atop the Duke of York steps. The Column is 124 feet tall and the total cost was £25,000. The Grand ol' Duke, the second son of George III, was the famous commander-in-chief of the army celebrated in rhyme. The cost of his monument was met by stopping one day's pay from each soldier in the army (Weinreb and Hibbert, 1983; 240). For Nowell this highly visible and prestigious project must have represented a major challenge since the column was to be constructed of Yorkshire stone slabs for the base courses, Aberdeenshire grey granite for the pediment, and Peterhead red granite for the shaft and upper pedestal. It is hard to imagine a greater contrast in texture and hardness to the Bath stone Philip had been used to until now. The payment to Philip Nowell was a massive £15,760 9s. 6d. including, of course, the cost of stone. Contemporary commentators regarded this sum fully justified, however, since the work was accomplished in just twenty months, a full four months ahead of schedule, and by a *"builder who fully understood [the architect's] designs, and worked up to them in a tradesman-like manner"* (Robertson, 1834). The project was completed early in 1834, and for the next few years he continued to work from his base at Grosvenor Wharf in Lower Belgrave Place; no doubt continuing to build houses using the now fashionable Bath Stone. In 1838 Philip, accompanied by his son, Philip Nowell the Younger, was employed once more by the Duke of Wellington for work on alterations to the Duke's home at Stratfield Saye, near Reading, also using Bath stone (Gunnis,1951; 282). Shortly afterwards, Philip was to begin work on his own memorial.

The 'West of London and Westminster Cemetery Co.' was floated in 1836. In a rapidly expanding metropolis such as London finding space for burial of the dead was a major problem after small parish churchyards became full. Thus, in the 1830s a number of private companies were founded to purchase space at the edge of the city to 'build' a cemetery. Those who could afford the fees could then buy plots from the Company for their own burial. Highgate is perhaps the best known of these cemeteries. The West of London Company established Brompton Cemetery, in Kensington, the 40 acre site being acquired in 1838. A competition was then launched for an architectural plan which would allow Brompton to match, even outshine rivals such as Highgate. At that time Highgate was not only *the* place to be seen buried, but had also become a popular attraction for weekend promenaders (Weinreb and Hibbert, 1983; 380). After all, as private companies, the cemeteries were themselves in competition with one another for business. The competition judge was to be Sir Jeffrey Wyattville. This was actually Jeffrey Wyatt, Philip Nowell's old friend, who had changed his name when he was knighted by George IV after completion of the Windsor Castle project. The winner was a young pupil of Wyattville named Benjamin Baud. With ironic sensibility, shortly after the judgment was declared, Jeffrey Wyattville died. Baud, following his masters' tradition, appointed Philip Nowell as master mason.

The winning design was based on the plan of a vast cathedral. The central, Anglican chapel was a large, domed, octagonal structure from which burial vaults were arranged as if they were the spokes of a giant wheel. The Chapel was to be built of Bath stone, and the estimated cost was the huge sum of £30,000. Things soon began to go badly wrong, however, with fewer than expected subscribers, and troubles encountered with the building design. In 1841 shareholders were informed that £61,000 had been spent already on the incomplete works, and that Philip Nowell himself had kept the project going by advancing large sums of money to the Company.

The management also began to notice structural defects, which led to the builder and the architect accusing each other. The directors owed so much to Nowell that they naturally took his side and Baud was dismissed, leading him to sue the Company, but he was unsuccessful...

(www.brompton.org/History.htm).

In 1852, partly due to continuing financial difficulty, and partly because the Authorities felt there was insufficient burial space for those less well-off, the cemetery was bought by the General Board of Health. This purchase is said to have been the first example ever of a private company becoming nationalized. Whatever Philip thought of this he could not yet 'turn in his grave'. He did not die until the following year, probably at Rock Hall, and was then interred at Brompton. His tomb, appropriately is of the 'Gothic shrine' type.

The Byfield Legacy

During the heyday of Royal and noble patronage for major building works in the 1820s and 1830s Philip Nowell emerged as the pre-eminent mason and supplier for Bath stone. His close connection with the Byfield Mine meant that, inevitably, these works would have a major impact on the Combe Down landscape.

Supply of stone for the Windsor Castle project had exhausted Nowell's Rock Hall quarry. By 1828 it was empty of valuable free-stone. It seems, however, that Philip returned to Combe Down for a while to sort out future affairs since from this time onwards his name is recorded with more clarity and regularity in the Parish Rate Books than it had been previously. As 'owner' of the quarry he would first have to ensure the site was leveled, then covered with topsoil to make it suitable for cultivation. Some time after 1828 the site was leased to James Cambridge, a tenant who lived in the lower of the Rock Hall Cottages (no. 6) and who was already farming other Nowell property. In 1837 he was charged extra rates, for the first time, for just over two acres of '*land*', suggesting this was the year he succeeded in cultivating market garden produce on the old quarry site (LW Parish Rate Books). In 1841 the Population Census described him as a '*yeoman*', aged 70.

Philip Nowell also seems to have drawn up plans at this time for his own house. The fact he had renamed the quarry 'Rock Hall' some years earlier indicates it had long been his dream to build a fine home here for himself, perhaps with his eventual retirement in mind. Actual construction of Rock Hall probably began in 1829, and for the first time we are given an idea of Nowell's very own tastes in building design, unhindered by the fancies and foibles of a 'qualified' architect. Unfortunately subsequent 20th century construction obscures the original context of Rock Hall, but contemporary descriptions and early photographs do offer some clues. Most importantly, Nowell's close attachment to his family is confirmed by the fact he designed his home as an extension to his father's house, rather than as a detached residence. Samuel Nowell's house, then occupied by Philip's elder brother, also called Sam, was a simple cottage design, albeit three stories tall. This is the building known as 'Rock Hall Cottage' in subsequent Census records. Philip's 'Hall' was the same height, but distinctly more Gothic in appearance.

All in all, he produced one of the oddest looking semi-detached pairings, not just on Combe Down, but anywhere in Bath and surrounding district (fig 15).

Rock Hall was not the only new residence to be constructed at this time. According to the Parish Rate Books the number of 'occupiers' of residences in the Combe Down part of Lyncombe and Widcombe doubled between 1827 and 1831, from 23 to 46 (LW Parish Rate Books). On the Nowell 'estate', Philip's younger brother Jacob, also a mason, began to build some cottages. The new buildings were modern-day nos. 1&2 and 4&5 Rock Hall Cottages. The 'mystery' surrounding No. 3 remains unresolved, though the potential for confusion with *the* Rock Hall Cottage is obvious and may explain why the gap in the sequence occurs. Jacob's own residence was one of these new homes, although it seems to have moved according to whichever was under construction at the time when rates were collected, just as in his father's day. By the time of the Population Census in 1841 Jacob seems to have settled in No. 2. A year or two later his son, also named Jacob, entered the Rudman household as apprentice mason/quarryman and appears as such in the 1851 Census records, aged 18.

The new residents in the other Rock Hall cottages all seem to have been closely connected with the stone trade. One was a quarryman, another was a mason, and the other a waggoner; and all were there despite the fact the Nowell quarry had by now been worked out. Elsewhere on the Down the terrace of cottages along Greendown Place was also constructed at this time, effectively reclaiming another stretch of former quarry ground. This was on land which had previously formed part of Henry Street's quarry, but which now was filled and compacted with discard. Henry Street, meanwhile, continued to push forward his quarry-faces, both above and below ground, for so long as the orders for stone continued to flow. Certainly Philip Nowell would have spent much of his time in Combe Down assessing the potential of the remaining Byfield quarries, with a mind on fulfilling future contracts that might come his way. He was surely confident that major works were in the offing and that only the best stone, and the best quarries, operated perhaps by his best friends, with the best set of gangers and men, were to be obtained here at Byfield.

By 1831, with Nowell continuing to receive major new building contracts the quarrymasters of Byfield must have believed that the good times were all set to continue. For John Scrace, however, time was up. Apart from William Hulonce, who had ceased quarrying in 1826/7, Scrace had been left with the smallest of the quarry stakes after Street purchased the late Abraham Sumsion's plot in 1809. The Rate Books imply that Scrace not only gave up quarrying in 1831, but also died that year – or shortly afterwards. If Nowell did indeed still purchase Byfield stone it must have been from either Sophia Rudman or Henry Street. Since both quarry operations were virtually contiguous with the former Nowell quarry, the quality of stone could be reasonably assured. More quarrymen might have been taken on, and efforts may have been made even to improve conditions of work. By the time Nowell had completed the Duke of York's Column in 1834, it seems Philip Nowell was being feted as something of a local hero. Within Combe Down people took to calling him 'Sir Philip' and he is still remembered thus according to some local histories (e.g. Combe Down Townswomen's Guild, 1965). What is the truth of this? Was Philip Nowell really dubbed by the King's sword?

In 1828, the architect Jeffrey Wyatt was knighted by King George IV and received royal consent to change his name. He was allowed to become Sir Jeffrey Wyattville, on account of his services to architecture and, in particular, his recent works on the re-shaping of Windsor Castle. (It was also a means for him to be distinguished from the numerous other architect members of his family.) Philip Nowell was but one mason working on the walls of the Castle; other craftsmen applying their own specialist skills to other stones, such as Kentish Rag, also used in the project. He may have commanded the King's attention, but as yet his stature was insufficient to be awarded further respect. Construction of the Duke of York's Column would have been a different issue. Philip was *the* master mason. This was *his* work, albeit following the instructions of an architect. The work commemorated a man who was elder brother to the present King – a man who would have inherited the monarchy but for his untimely and premature death – a man who could otherwise have saved William IV the onerous task of ruling the nation. On this occasion it is indeed conceivable that the King not only recognized Nowell's contribution to the fabric of the landscape of London, but also offered appropriate reward. At that time, during the reigns of both George IV and his brother William IV, the most appropriate award was often deemed to be the Guelphic Order of Knighthood. The many British recipients of this medal would have been reminded that the Order had been founded by the Prince Regent in 1815 in honour of the Hanoverians who had served at Waterloo. 'Puffing (King William IV) Billy' was fond of using this award for distribution to worthies but, within a few short years, by the time of Queen Victoria, the Order had fallen from favour. Nominees were never entered on the Rolls, and so cannot be traced today. Let us assume Philip was indeed dubbed a Knight – but it is unlikely we shall ever know for sure.

Whatever the bureaucratic muddle regarding Philip Nowell's status in the eyes of the monarch it seems clear that the locals of Combe Down were in no doubt. Job Salter's *'house and brewery'*, founded in 1824, was quite possibly known in its early days by the simple name of 'Salter's'. In the early 1830s the name of the pub was changed to The King William, and later, presumably on the occasion of his death in 1837, to King William IV (LW Parish Rate Books). This name change surely recognized a mark of respect felt by the local community towards a monarch who not only provided the means to well-being for the workers in the stone mines, but who also offered royal recognition to the mason who had helped bring Bath stone to national attention.

Sophia Rudman seems to have passed on responsibility for her quarry to her son John in 1833 (when they are listed jointly in the Rate Books), and to have died within the next few years. In 1836 the Rudmans ceased paying quarry rates, suggesting this quarry too had become worked out. Now, only the Street Quarry was left in operation. This is confirmed, in a sense, by William Smith, who made a final visit to Combe Down in 1838 whilst touring the country as a member of the four-man Commission appointed to seek the best stone for building the new Houses of Parliament. His diary entry for September 30th reads:

About the Abbey and the Churches in Bath. To Combe Down Free-Stone quarries - through Stoke Wolverton, Frome, & Nunny to Doulting Quarries and Shepton Mallet & Wells.

(Smith Papers, Univ. of Oxford Museum Library)

In their final report, published a year later, the Commissioners indicate that they had visited 'Lodge Hill' Quarry, operated by Isaac Sumsion, and that this was one of only six quarries still in operation on Combe Down. The 1841 Population Census confirms that there were only six quarrymasters in the village in that year, and that the only one operating in the Byfield area was Henry Street. It is a shame that William Smith could not afford to pay his old friend a visit. Did Smith's own quarry failure and subsequent bankruptcy have something to do with this? Had Smith gone against Street's good advice? After all, Henry Street had now proven to be the most enduring of the Byfield quarrymasters. Or, was Street perhaps under contract already to provide stone for other projects, such as Nowell's works at Brompton Cemetery?

The other four quarrymasters included George Davidge (son of John – former quarryman and now 'publican') another Isaac Sumsion, and James Ford. All lived in or near Combe Down village centre, and probably worked the surviving remnants of the original Allen quarries associated with the Firs Mine. Also named as quarrymaster in the Census is William Stennard who, along with Isaac Sumsion Senior, was almost certainly exploiting the quarry grounds just to the east of the village – between Shaft Road and Mount Pleasant. It is these men, together with Henry Street, who may have felt most threatened by the newly exposed beds of Bath Stone 'discovered' during construction of the Box Tunnel on the Great Western Railway in 1840. They need not have feared, however. Any signs of recent decline in the industry on Combe Down can be attributed to the simple fact that quarries had recently ceased operations because high demand for Bath Stone meant they had become worked out. Box Stone, which often had rather different weathering and structural characteristics to Combe Down Stone, could be transported to London directly by rail, and at cheaper cost because of better accessibility. The impact of this development seems to have been merely to fuel the demand for Bath Stone. As a result the number of quarries in Combe Down began to *increase* after 1840 when new grounds were opened up on the north side of Bradford Road. The 1851 Monkton Combe Tithe Survey records that at least one Isaac Sumsion had moved or established here, and also William Stennard, together with at least three 'newcomers' – including a Richard Lankesheer. The most likely loser in this process was Philip Nowell. As rail transportation became more popular, so reliance on the canal barge diminished. From 1840 onwards it seems likely that Nowell's yard and wharf on the Grosvenor Canal saw less and less business. Eventually, by 1861, the railway had proved truly dominant. The Grosvenor Canal Basin was filled in to become part of the foundation for the new Victoria Station (Barker and Jackson, 1990; 123).

In 1850 Philip Nowell finally returned to Combe Down to live in Rock Hall. His first wife, Ann, had died and now, at the age of 70, he decided to remarry. His bride was Harriet Street, aged 34, who was the eldest daughter of Henry Street Junior. Henry himself seems to have used this opportunity to also retire from the world of quarrying – and so he sold all his quarry interests. The purchaser was Philip Nowell – who now became owner of all surviving fragments of the Byfield Mine.

We do not know the precise details of the agreement made between Philip Nowell and Henry Street, but there is nothing to indicate that the arrangement was anything other than an entirely amicable one. The whole affair seems to suggest that the relationship between these men was close in both a business sense as well as in personal friendship. Philip's will was changed to make allowance for the possibility that he might sire more children (Bath City Archives). In the meantime he bequeathed that Rock Hall and the surrounding Estate, including the quarries acquired from Henry Street, should be held in trust and that all income accruing should be for the benefit and maintenance of his widow, Harriet. The Trustees were to be his surviving sons; Philip the Younger and Arthur Nowell. Philip the Elder died without further issue on 14th February, 1853 at the age of 73.

Immediately after Philip's death his sons (executors and trustees) sold the northernmost plots of the quarries which had formerly belonged to Henry Street, including the original Widcombe Field Quarry, all of which had long since been infilled and developed for housing (Private deeds). This would have provided some capital for Harriet, although regular income would also come from the quarry and plantation which were still producing stone and timber for the building industry. The quarry included Patrick Byrne's former workings and also part of the underground quarry in LW Byfield. It is clear that neither Harriet nor Philip's sons engaged in any quarrying themselves here, and the presumption must be that they employed a ganger to do the work for them. There is intriguing evidence that Henry Street may have still been involved supervising quarry operations. Another of the sales that Philip the Younger conducted after his father's death (Arthur also died in 1853) was numbers 1 and 2 Rock Hall Cottages. Nowell's share of Ralph Allen's Yard was also included in this sale. The purchaser was Henry Street (Bath City Archives, MH/11/3-8) and the occupant was Jacob Nowell, now aged about 40. Is it possible that Street 'supervised' the quarry operations, the proceeds of which would go to his daughter, and that Jacob Nowell was hired as his ganger? Throughout Harriet's lifetime the quarry continued to be known as Street's Quarry, as evidenced by the 'Particulars and Conditions of Sale' when the estate was put up for auction in 1883 (Bath City Archives, MH/11/1). Jacob Nowell, for his part, was described as a '*mason*' in the 1841 Population Census, and as a '*quarryman*' in 1851 and 1861. In 1871 he is given the intriguing title of '*quarrymason*'.

In 1857 Henry Street sold the cottages and his share of Ralph Allen's Yard to Henry Morrish, the well-known 'Wine and Spirit Merchant' of Bath. In 1851 Morrish had acquired the fragments that remained of William Hulonce's land by paying off the mortgage still owed to James Gooden (£413 15s. 2d.), and formed a partnership with Thomas Hine who had taken over the King William IV public house (Bath City Archives, MH/7/14). Together they planned an expansion of the pub into "Combe Down Brewery", and the 1857 purchase of Ralph Allen's Yard allowed them to construct the malthouse which now constitutes the yard buildings. In 1861 Moorish also purchased the old Rudman quarry from John Rudman, grandson of Jonathan and Sophia, who still lived in the original Rudman cottage. The entire site, now measuring 2 acres 2 roods and 25 perches, including the cottage, was sold for a paltry £100. John Rudman signed the contract with his mark – an 'X'. The cottage was remodeled into a fashionable south-facing villa for the benefit and comfort of Morrish and his family. This building is now known as Tor View, and the fact that 'JxN' is scratched into one of the walls suggests that Jacob Nowell was the mason in charge. All this development meant, of course, that Ralph Allen's Yard could no longer be used as a quarry entrance, and that underground working had effectively ceased.

The break-up of the Nowell estate occurred because both Arthur (died 1853) and Philip the Younger (died 1871) pre-deceased their step-mother, Harriet, who died in 1879. As trustees of the estate they had failed, in their own wills, to make provision for the appointment of new trustees, or to give any indication of how the estate should be managed after Harriet's death. Not surprisingly, different branches of the family laid claim to Rock Hall and the surrounding estate and the issue came to the High Court for resolution. The order was given that the estate should be put up for auction so the income could be divided among the family members. Rock Hall itself eventually was acquired by the Trustees of Magdelen Hospital for use as a Hospital for Imbecile Children. Street's Quarry was sold as a separate lot, and eventually acquired by a gentleman by the name of Augustus Thatcher Cox, a grocer of Combe Cottage, Combe Down. Remarkably little is known of this man, except that his property dealings took place mostly in the 1920s according to local deeds. Nevertheless, it is he who gave the name to Cox's Quarry, as Street's Quarry became known for most of the 20th century (Addison, 1998). Almost certainly he did not quarry himself, but employed a ganger to do the work for him. Interestingly, local oral tradition provides a clue to explain why this quarry lasted so long, for people recall *three* discrete layers of freestone being exposed here. Cox's quarry ceased operations in 1967 and was taken over by Beazer's Co. as a dump for building waste. It has now reverted to residential land.

Access to the underground sections of the old Byfield Mine is now severely restricted. In any case work is now underway to infill the caverns. For many years, however, access was open from many private properties, and from time to time local newspapers would carry stories of people becoming lost in the intricate maze of pitch-dark chambers and passageways. Ultimately it is the safety issue which not only caused the mines to be sealed, but which has sealed their ultimate fate. It is somewhat ironic therefore, to reflect on the time when Byfield Mine was last used by the local community. During the Bath air raids in April, 1942, more than two hundred people filed down the incline originally excavated by William Hulonce to seek shelter from the bombs. They each paid a penny to cover the cost of electricity which was run down by cable from Tor View, and heating was provided by charcoal brazier. Thus, the last recorded use of the underground sections of the Byfield Mine was as a safe haven for the people of Combe Down from the dangers which threatened from above!

Bibliography

Addison, Peter (1998), *Around Combe Down*. Millstream Books; Bath.

Barker, Felix; and Jackson, Peter (1990), *The History of London in Maps*. Barrie & Jenkins; London.

Beazer, Cyril H.G. (1981), *Random Reflections of a West Country Craftsman*. Beazer; Bath.

Berg, Maxine (1994), *The Age of Manufactures 1700-1820: Industry, Innovation and Work in Britain (2nd Edition)*. Routledge; London.

Boyce, Benjamin (1967), *A Benevolent Man: A Life of Ralph Allen of Bath*. Harvard Univ. Press; Cambridge, Mass.

Burnett, David (1978), *Longleat: The Story of an English Country House*. Collins; London.

Chapman, Mike (1996), *A Guide to the Estates of Ralph Allen Around Bath*. Survey of Old Bath; Bath.

Chapman, Mike; Hawkes, John; and Holland, Elizabeth (1998), *The J. Charlton Map of Lyncombe and Widcombe, 1799*. Survey of Old Bath; Bath.

Devon, Elizabeth; Parkins, John; Workman, David (2001), *Bath in Stone: A Guide to the City's Building Stones*. Bath Geological Society; Bath.

Gunnis, Rupert (1951), *Dictionary of British Sculptors, 1660-1851 (Revised edition)*. Abbey Library; London.

Oxford Archaeology (2004), *Combe Down Stone Mines, Bath, Stabilisation Project. Emergency Works Archaeological Recording Action. Interim Report April 2001 – December 2003*. Oxford Archaeology, Oxford.

Pevsner, Niklaus (1957), *The Buildings of England: London Volume 1 – The Cities of London and Westminster*. Penguin; London.

Pollard, David (1994), *Historical and Archaeological Assessment of the Underground Quarries Now Known as Firs Mine and Byfield Mine*. B&NES.

Robinson, John (2000), *Buckingham Palace: The Official Illustrated History*. The Royal Collection; London.

Robertson, J. (1834), *"A Descriptive Account of the Duke of York's Monument, accompanied by Plans, Elevations, and Sections, copied from the Designs of Benjamin Wyatt, Esq., Architect"*. Architectural Magazine, 1834.

Sellar, W.C. and Yeatman R.J. (1930), *1066 And All That*. Methuen; London.

Willies, Lynn in Parsons Brinkerhoff Ltd (2002), *Combe Down Stabilisation Project – Phase 1. Environmental Assessment of Options*. For BANES.

Winchester, Simon (2001), *The Map That Changed the World*. Penguin Books; London.

Weinreb, Ben; and Hibbert, Christopher (eds.) (1983), *The London Encyclopaedia*. Macmillan; London.

Wooster, Philip (1978), *"The Stone Industry at Bath"*. Bristol Industrial Archaeological Society Journal, Vol. II, 1978.

Workman, David (2003), *"The Use of Bath Stone: A Potted History"*. Bath Geological Society Journal. Autumn, 2003.